Good Food magazine

101 SEASONAL SALADS

First published 2005
Published by BBC Books, an imprint of Ebury Publishing

10 9 8 7

Ebury Publishing is a division of the Random House Group Ltd.

The Random House Group Ltd Reg. No. 954009

Addresses for companies within the Random House Group Ltd can be
found at www.randomhouse.co.uk

A CIP catalogue record for this book is available from the British Library.

The Random House Group Ltd makes every effort to ensure that the
papers used in our books are made from trees that have been legally
sourced from well-managed and credibly certified forests. Our paper
procurement policy can be found at www.randomhouse.co.uk

Commissioning Editor: Vivien Bowler
Project Editor: Sarah Reece
Project Co-ordinator for *BBC Good Food Magazine*: Sarah Sysum
Designer: Kathryn Gammon
Production Controller: Peter Hunt

Set in Bookman Old Style, Helvetica and ITC Officina Sans
Printed and bound in Italy by LEGO SpA
Colour origination by Butler & Tanner, Frome, England

ISBN 978 0 563 52221 8

101 SEASONAL SALADS
TRIED-AND-TESTED RECIPES

Editor
Angela Nilsen

BOOKS

Contents

Introduction   6

Introduction

Salads have never been so exciting and imaginative. We are spoilt for choice with the wonderful array of leaves and herbs that greet us in supermarkets. But salads aren't just about combining different leaves for a simple side order – we are enjoying them more and more in amazing combinations as the main event – even dessert.

To show just how versatile a salad can be, we at *BBC Good Food Magazine* have picked out over 100 of our favourites, including the *Exotic Avocado Salad* pictured opposite (see page 150 for recipe). Intriguing ingredients and flavours have been mixed and matched, marinated and tossed, to create all-year-round salad recipes that can be quickly assembled for any scenario, be it a mid-week supper or something more fancy.

As always, all the recipes have been thoroughly tested in the *Good Food* kitchen to bring you the most practical, delicious-tasting food we can. Plus, each one has a nutritional breakdown, so you can keep an eye on the calorie, fat and salt content. With this unique collection by your side, you'll have loads of stylish salad ideas – so easy to throw together for family or friends.

Angela Nilsen

Angela Nilsen
BBC Good Food Magazine

Conversion tables

NOTES ON THE RECIPES
• Eggs are medium in the UK and Australia (large in America) unless stated otherwise.
• Wash all fresh produce before preparation.

OVEN TEMPERATURES

Gas	°C	Fan °C	°F	Oven temp.
¼	110	90	225	Very cool
½	120	100	250	Very cool
1	140	120	275	Cool or slow
2	150	130	300	Cool or slow
3	160	140	325	Warm
4	180	160	350	Moderate
5	190	170	375	Moderately hot
6	200	180	400	Fairly hot
7	220	200	425	Hot
8	230	210	450	Very hot
9	240	220	475	Very hot

APPROXIMATE WEIGHT CONVERSIONS
• All the recipes in this book list both imperial and metric measurements. Conversions are approximate and have been rounded up or down. Follow one set of measurements only; do not mix the two.
• Cup measurements, which are used by cooks in Australia and America, have not been listed here as they vary from ingredient to ingredient. Please use kitchen scales to measure dry/solid ingredients.

SPOON MEASURES

- Spoon measurements are level unless otherwise specified.
- 1 teaspoon = 5ml
- 1 tablespoon = 15ml
- 1 Australian tablespoon = 20ml (cooks in Australia should measure 3 teaspoons where 1 tablespoon is specified in a recipe)

APPROXIMATE LIQUID CONVERSIONS

metric	imperial	AUS	US
50ml	2fl oz	¼ cup	¼ cup
125ml	4fl oz	½ cup	½ cup
175ml	6fl oz	¾ cup	¾ cup
225ml	8fl oz	1 cup	1 cup
300ml	10fl oz/½ pint	½ pint	1¼ cups
450ml	16fl oz	2 cups	2 cups/1 pint
600ml	20fl oz/1 pint	1 pint	2½ cups
1 litre	35fl oz/1¾ pints	1¾ pints	1 quart

Serve as soon as you've spooned over the dressing or the salad will wilt.

Crispy Parma Ham with Avocado and Hot Tomato Dressing

5 tbsp olive oil, plus extra for drizzling
85g/3oz Parma ham, roughly torn
2 large plum tomatoes, quartered, seeded and cut into thin slivers
1 small bunch basil, roughly chopped
juice of 1 lemon
100–120g bag mixed salad leaves, such as rocket, spinach and watercress
1 large ripe avocado, peeled and sliced

Takes 5 minutes • Serves 4

1 Heat 1 tablespoon of the oil in a non-stick frying pan over a high heat. Fry the Parma ham pieces, half at a time, seasoned with pepper, for 1 minute on each side until crisp. Keep warm.

2 Using kitchen paper, wipe out the excess fat from the frying pan and return to a low heat. Heat the remaining oil, then add the tomatoes, basil and lemon juice. Season with pepper and gently heat through for about 30 seconds.

3 Arrange the salad leaves on four serving plates. Top with the avocado slices, then the crispy pieces of ham. Spoon over the hot dressing and serve at once. Drizzle with a little extra olive oil if you like.

• Per serving 269 kcalories, protein 7g, carbohydrate 3g, fat 25g, saturated fat 4g, fibre 2g, added sugar none, salt 1.1g

You can prepare the salad and dressing a few hours ahead, but do the eggs, the lardons and the tossing together just before serving.

Salade aux Lardons

6 tbsp olive oil
1 tsp Dijon mustard
2 × 120g bags prepared mixed baby green salad leaves (or make your own mix of curly endive, chicory and spinach)
6 free-range eggs, at room temperature
130g pack lardons or diced pancetta
2 tbsp red wine vinegar
French-style bread, to serve

Takes 25 minutes • Serves 6

1 Mix the olive oil and mustard in a salad bowl and season. Tip the salad leaves into the bowl on top of the salad servers to protect them from the dressing. Don't toss.
2 Boil the eggs in a pan of boiling water for 7 minutes until softly set. Drain and refresh under cold water, leave until cool enough to handle, then peel off the shells.
3 Dry fry the lardons or pancetta in a non-stick frying pan for 3 minutes until crisp and golden. Tip them over the leaves. Swirl the vinegar into the pan, then drizzle over the salad. Toss the salad and divide between six plates. Halve each egg and put two halves on each salad. Serve immediately, with bread.

• Per serving 263 kcalories, protein 12g, carbohydrate 1g, fat 23g, saturated fat 6g, fibre none, added sugar none, salt 1.07g

Get everything ready and sizzle the bacon and liver as guests sit down for a quick lunch or supper.

Warm Chicken Liver Salad

142g jar roasted peppers in olive oil, drained and cut into strips
2 × 40g packs lamb's lettuce
25g/1oz plain flour
400g/14oz chicken livers, trimmed and thinly sliced
4 rashers streaky bacon, coarsely chopped
2 tbsp olive oil
2 tsp red wine vinegar

Takes 15 minutes • Serves 4

1 Toss the strips of pepper with the lettuce and divide into piles between four plates. Season the flour and use it to coat the chicken livers.

2 Heat a frying pan and add the chopped bacon. Dry fry until crisp, then remove and set aside on kitchen paper. Heat the oil in the pan and fry the chicken livers for 30 seconds–1 minute on each side. Remove from the heat and stir in the red wine vinegar.

3 Arrange the chicken livers on the lamb's lettuce and peppers. Scatter over the bacon, drizzle over the dressing from the pan, season with black pepper and serve immediately.

• Per serving 257 kcalories, protein 23g, carbohydrate 7g, fat 15g, saturated fat 4g, fibre 1g, added sugar none, salt 1g

Add the nuts to this healthy and simple salad at the last minute, so that they remain crunchy.

Artichoke and Lemon Salad

3 lemons, plus a squeeze to taste
2 tbsp rock salt
1 tbsp fresh thyme leaves
2 tbsp clear honey
1 tbsp red wine vinegar
5 tbsp extra virgin olive oil
2 × 400g cans artichoke hearts in salted water, rinsed and halved
3 × 70–90g packs sliced Italian meats, such as prosciutto, bresaola and salami
50g bag rocket
140g/5oz blanched roasted almonds

Takes 40 minutes • Serves 6

1 Put 2 whole lemons into a saucepan of water with the rock salt and simmer, well submerged, for 10 minutes until soft. Tip the lemons into a sieve and cool under the cold tap.

2 Mix the thyme with the honey, vinegar and olive oil. Squeeze the juice from the remaining lemon and add to the honey mixture.

3 Halve the boiled lemons, trim away all the flesh and membranes and remove the bitter white pith from the inside of the skin. Finely chop the remaining thin pieces of lemon skin and toss them into the dressing with the artichokes. Pile into a serving dish. Arrange the meats on a platter. Toss the rocket into the salad with the roasted almonds.

• Per serving 432 kcalories, protein 21g, carbohydrate 12g, fat 32g, saturated fat 6g, fibre 4g, added sugar 4g, salt 2.78g

Make the most of cep mushrooms throughout the autumn
with this delicious salad.

Cep and Parmesan Salad

200g/8oz small firm ceps
2 tbsp lemon juice
5 tbsp extra virgin olive oil
50g bag rocket
100g/4oz parmesan cheese
shavings

Takes 20 minutes • Serves 4

1 Carefully wipe the ceps with damp kitchen paper. Finely slice, then lay them flat on a large plate. Mix the lemon juice with 2 teaspoons water and some seasoning, then whisk in the olive oil.
2 Brush about half of the dressing over the mushrooms with a pastry brush, then season. Marinate for about 10 minutes.
3 Toss the rocket and parmesan shavings with the rest of the dressing and season. Divide between four plates and gently place the ceps on top.

• Per serving 235 kcalories, protein 10g, carbohydrate 1g, fat 21g, saturated fat 6.6g, fibre 0.2g, added sugar none, salt 0.58g

Assemble everything on the baking sheet and it's ready for the oven at a moment's notice.

Baked Figs and Goat's Cheese

6 figs
200g/8oz soft goat's cheese, sliced
1 head radicchio
85g/3oz walnut pieces

FOR THE DRESSING
6 tbsp olive oil
3 tbsp balsamic vinegar

Takes 30 minutes • Serves 6

1 Preheat the oven to 180°C/Gas 4/fan oven 160°C. Cut the figs into quarters, from the top almost to the base, and lay them on a non-stick baking sheet (or one lined with foil and oiled). Put the goat's cheese in the centre of the figs.
2 Bake for 10–15 minutes until the cheese is melted and tinged brown. Meanwhile, whisk the dressing ingredients with some seasoning.
3 Put a couple of good radicchio leaves on each serving plate and lay the warm figs on top. Scatter with the walnuts and drizzle with the dressing. Serve warm or at room temperature.

• Per serving 314 kcalories, protein 8g, carbohydrate 7g, fat 28g, saturated fat 7g, fibre 2g, added sugar none, salt 0.81g

Wasabi, used to add a hot peppery bite to sushi, peps up this mild and creamy combination of avocado and prawns.

Avocado Prawns in Wasabi Dressing

FOR THE DRESSING
2 tsp wasabi paste
4 tbsp olive oil
2 tbsp lime juice
1 tsp clear honey

FOR THE SALAD
2 large ripe but firm avocados
250g pack large cooked peeled prawns
2 heads chicory, red if possible, separated into leaves
few sprigs of watercress
6 lime wedges

Takes 15 minutes • Serves 6

1 In a large bowl, mix the dressing ingredients until blended. Season with salt, then set aside.
2 Halve and stone the avocados. Dice the flesh while it's still in the skin, then scoop it into a bowl. Add the prawns and dressing and toss together.
3 Line six small serving bowls or tumblers with two or three chicory leaves. Pile in the avocado and prawn mixture. Top with watercress sprigs and lime wedges.

• Per serving 223 kcalories, protein 11g, carbohydrate 3g, fat 19g, saturated fat 2g, fibre 2g, added sugar 1g, salt 1.71g

This speedy salad makes a light and colourful starter for a buffet and can be prepared ahead, then assembled in minutes.

Seared Honeyed Salmon

1 tbsp olive oil
450g/1lb piece salmon fillet, skinned
2 large oranges
3 small red onions
200g/8oz large cooked peeled prawns
2 × 150g bags mixed salad leaves

FOR THE DRESSING
125ml/4fl oz olive oil
2 tbsp wholegrain mustard
1½ tbsp heather or clear honey
1 tbsp mayonnaise
1 tbsp white wine vinegar or raspberry vinegar

Takes 30 minutes • Serves 8

1 Heat 1 tablespoon oil in a non-stick frying pan. Cook the salmon, skinned side down, for 12–15 minutes, turning halfway through, until cooked and opaque in the centre. Meanwhile, whizz all the dressing ingredients with some seasoning in a blender.

2 Peel and segment the oranges and remove any pith (work over a plate to catch the juices). Stir the orange juice into the dressing. Slice the onions. Flake the salmon into large pieces, then spoon half the dressing over it.

3 To serve, put the sliced onions, prawns and orange segments in a large bowl and drizzle over the remaining dressing. Toss in the salad leaves. Lift the mixture on to a platter and scatter over the salmon flakes. Season with pepper and serve immediately.

• Per serving 326 kcalories, protein 19g, carbohydrate 9g, fat 24g, saturated fat 4g, fibre 2g, added sugar 2g, salt 1.79g

This is a Chilean dish of Spanish origin that is usually based on lime juice or vinegar mixed with onions, pepper and spices.

Spiced Prawn and Avocado Salad

juice of 3 limes
5 spring onions, thinly sliced
1 tbsp tomato paste
large pinch dried oregano
300g/10oz ripe tomatoes, cherry or plum, finely chopped
1 green chilli, seeded and finely chopped
400g pack large frozen cooked peeled prawns, defrosted
2 ripe avocados
3 tbsp chopped coriander
iceberg lettuce leaves and ready-cooked poppadums, to serve

Takes 25 minutes • Serves 8

1 In a non-metallic bowl, mix the lime juice, spring onions, tomato paste, oregano, tomatoes and chilli. Mix well and season.
2 Pat the prawns dry with kitchen paper. Peel, stone and cube the avocados. Add the prawns, avocados and coriander to the tomato mixture and mix well. (This can be done up to 3 hours ahead.)
3 Carefully separate the lettuce leaves and arrange them over a serving platter. Spoon the prawn mixture into the cup-shaped leaves and serve with crisp ready-cooked poppadums.

• Per serving 134 kcalories, protein 12g, carbohydrate 2g, fat 8g, saturated fat 1.5g, fibre 1.5g, added sugar none, salt 1.9g

A simple, low-fat salad
that makes a great starter.

Watermelon and Prawn Salad

juice of 3 limes and 1½ oranges
1 garlic clove
handful of coriander stems
1 tsp golden caster sugar
1 red chilli, seeded, plus 1 tsp
chopped to garnish
6cm/2½in piece of fresh root ginger,
peeled
1 small watermelon, weighing about
1.8kg/4lb
24 large cooked peeled tiger prawns
4 spring onions, finely sliced
2 trimmed lemongrass stalks,
finely sliced
chopped coriander and mint leaves,
and roasted peanuts, to serve

Takes 45 minutes • Serves 6

1 Make the dressing. Remove the zest from one of the limes and set aside. Juice all the limes and oranges. Put the garlic and coriander stems in a food processor with 1 teaspoon salt and the sugar, then pulse to a pulp. Add the whole chilli, one third of the ginger, roughly chopped, and the citrus juices and pulse until smooth.
2 Cut the watermelon into segments, remove the skin and seed the flesh. Cut into lozenges about 3cm/1¼in wide. Cut the rest of the ginger into fine matchsticks.
3 Mix the melon and prawns and add the spring onions, lemongrass, the rest of the ginger and reserved lime zest. (This can be chilled for up to 2 hours.) Toss the dressing and chopped chilli into the salad and scatter with chopped coriander and mint and peanuts.

• Per serving 201 kcalories, protein 13g, carbohydrate 16g, fat 10g, saturated fat 2g, fibre 1g, added sugar 1g, salt 0.68g

Cooking raw prawns yourself gives juicier,
more flavoursome results than using ready-cooked ones.

Spicy Prawn Cocktail

350g/12oz raw peeled tiger prawns, thawed if frozen
1 garlic clove, finely chopped
1 red chilli, seeded and finely chopped
5 tbsp olive oil
2 vine tomatoes
1 tbsp lemon juice
1 tsp clear honey
1 tbsp chopped coriander
2 Little Gem lettuces
1 ripe avocado, peeled and stoned
handful of rocket leaves
Italian flatbread or toasted pittas, to serve

Takes 30 minutes, plus chilling • Serves 6

1 Pat the prawns dry with kitchen paper. Mix the garlic, chilli and prawns. Heat 1 tablespoon of the oil in a pan, add the prawns and stir fry for 2–3 minutes, until pink. (You can then chill the prawns for up to 8 hours.)

2 Meanwhile, quarter the tomatoes and discard the seeds. Finely chop the flesh and tip into a bowl with the lemon juice, honey and remaining oil. Add the coriander, season and whisk until slightly thickened. (You can then chill the tomato mixture for up to 8 hours.)

3 Tear the Little Gem leaves into small pieces. Chop the avocado flesh. Fill six glasses with the lettuce, avocado and rocket leaves. Pile the prawns on top and spoon over the tomato and coriander dressing. Serve with Italian flatbread or toasted pittas.

• Per serving 176 kcalories, protein 10g, carbohydrate 2g, fat 14g, saturated fat 2g, fibre 1g, added sugar 1g, salt 0.25g

You can replace the lemon juice with balsamic vinegar for a sharper taste.

Crispy Ham and Pear Salad

1 small cos lettuce
50g bag watercress or rocket
2 ripe avocados, peeled, stoned and sliced
handful of herbs, such as dill or chives
90g pack prosciutto
4 tbsp olive oil
2 ripe pears, cored and sliced
2 tsp wholegrain mustard
juice of ½ lemon

Takes 15 minutes • Serves 4

1 Tear the lettuce into bite-sized pieces, then arrange with the watercress or rocket, avocados and herbs on four large serving plates. Heat a large frying pan and fry the prosciutto until crisp. Lift out and set aside.
2 Heat the olive oil in the same pan. Add the pears, mustard and lemon juice and heat through briefly.
3 Return the prosciutto to the pan, season, then immediately spoon everything over the salad. Serve at once.

• Per serving 314 kcalories, protein 8g, carbohydrate 11g, fat 27g, saturated fat 4g, fibre 5g, added sugar none, salt 1.23g

This simple salad is packed with fresh flavours and tastes even better served in the garden in summer sunshine.

Greek Salad

1 medium red onion
1 tsp dried oregano
2 tbsp white wine vinegar
8 tbsp Greek extra virgin olive oil
4 ripe medium-sized tomatoes
1 cucumber
2 handfuls of kalamata black olives, pitted
leaves from 2 sprigs of fresh oregano, finely chopped
200g pack feta cheese

Takes 20 minutes, plus marinating • Serves 4

1 Halve and slice the onion, tip the slices into a bowl and sprinkle over the dried oregano. Stir in the vinegar and olive oil, cover and set aside for a couple of hours.
2 Cut the tomatoes into chunks. Quarter the cucumber lengthways and slice thickly across. Tip the tomatoes and cucumber into a salad bowl and add the onion, olives and half the fresh oregano. Season.
3 Crumble the feta roughly over the top of the salad and sprinkle with the remaining oregano. Stir together, taking care not to break up the feta.

• Per serving 369 kcalories, protein 10g, carbohydrate 7g, fat 34g, saturated fat 10g, fibre 2g, added sugar none, salt 2.58g

A stylish and unusual combination of smoked salmon and strawberries.

Salmon, Strawberry and Fennel Salad

200g pack smoked salmon, torn into strips
1 large bulb of fennel, trimmed, cored, halved and finely sliced into strips
50g bag rocket
200g/8oz ripe strawberries, hulled and halved
crusty brown rolls, to serve

FOR THE DRESSING
4 tbsp olive oil
2 tbsp white wine vinegar
2 tsp wholegrain mustard
1 tsp clear honey

Takes 15 minutes • Serves 4

1 In a small bowl, whisk together the dressing ingredients, season and set aside.
2 Put the smoked salmon, fennel, rocket and strawberries into a separate bowl.
3 Drizzle the dressing over the salad and toss gently so everything glistens. Finish with a grinding of black pepper and serve with crusty rolls.

• Per serving 198 kcalories, protein 14g, carbohydrate 5g, fat 14g, saturated fat 2g, fibre 2g, added sugar 1g, salt 2.52g

Turn a bag of salad into a quick and delicious midweek meal.

Smoked Mackerel with Crunchy Croûtons

2 thick slices crusty bread
1–2 tbsp olive oil
2 × 100g/4oz smoked mackerel fillets
150g bag mixed salad leaves, such as beetroot, lamb's lettuce and red chard
2–3 tbsp ready-made Caesar salad dressing

Takes 20 minutes • Serves 2

1 Preheat the oven to 200°C/Gas 6/fan oven 180°C. Cut the bread into cubes (no need to trim the crusts) and toss with the olive oil.
2 Spread the bread on to a baking sheet and bake for 15 minutes until crunchy and golden. Meanwhile, skin the mackerel fillets and tear the flesh into large flakes.
3 Toss the mackerel with the salad leaves, Caesar salad dressing and the warm croûtons, then serve.

• Per serving 582 kcalories, protein 23g, carbohydrate 22g, fat 45g, saturated fat 8.4g, fibre 1.3g, added sugar 0.2g, salt 2.82g

All the flavours of an Italian spring are here, with a couple of essential British ingredients.

Springtime Salad

550g/1¼lb new potatoes, scrubbed
800g/1¾lb young broad beans
in the pod (to give about
200g/8oz shelled beans)
200g/8oz fresh young asparagus
400g/14oz young peas in the pod
(to give about
100g/4oz shelled peas)
90g pack prosciutto, sliced
into ribbons
125g bag mixed salad leaves
100g/4oz pecorino cheese, shaved

FOR THE DRESSING
50g/2oz fresh watercress,
roughly chopped
6 tbsp extra virgin olive oil
2 tbsp cider vinegar
pinch sugar

Takes 35 minutes • Serves 4

1 Cook the potatoes in boiling salted water for 10–15 minutes until tender. Drain and halve. Blanch the shelled broad beans and the asparagus in boiling salted water for 2–3 minutes. Drain in a sieve and cool under running cold water. Drain again, fish out the asparagus, then peel off the outer skins of the beans. Blanch the shelled peas in a separate pan for 1 minute. Toss the asparagus with the beans, peas, potatoes and prosciutto.
2 Blitz all the dressing ingredients in a blender or food processor until smooth. Season.
3 Toss the salad leaves with a spoonful or two of dressing and arrange on plates. Pile the vegetable mix on top, season, then drizzle over the remaining dressing, scatter with the pecorino and serve.

• Per serving 493 kcalories, protein 25g, carbohydrate 31g, fat 31g, saturated fat 9g, fibre 7g, added sugar 0.5g, salt 1.57g

Mixing hot and cold ingredients creates an appetizing contrast of tastes and textures. Serve with a crusty baguette and a French dry white wine.

Warm Trout Salad with Dill

200g/8oz baby new potatoes, halved
125g pack smoked trout, flaked
50g/2oz mixed herb salad
few shreds of lemon zest

FOR THE VINAIGRETTE
5 tbsp olive oil
2 tsp tarragon vinegar or lemon juice
sliver of garlic, crushed
1 tbsp finely chopped fresh dill

FOR THE CREAM DRESSING
3 tbsp crème fraîche or double cream
1 tbsp lemon juice
1 tbsp finely chopped fresh dill

Takes 40 minutes • Serves 2

1 Cook the potatoes in salted boiling water for 8–10 minutes until tender. Meanwhile, mix the olive oil, vinegar, crushed garlic and seasoning for the vinaigrette, then mix in the dill. Drain the potatoes and return them to the pan. Spoon over 2 tablespoons of vinaigrette, cover the pan and keep warm.

2 Gently warm the crème fraîche or double cream, lemon juice and dill for the cream dressing in another (shallow) pan, stirring. Add the trout flakes and toss gently over a low heat until warm.

3 Scatter the salad and herb leaves and potatoes over two plates. Trickle over some of the remaining vinaigrette. Stir the lemon zest into the fish, then spoon the fish and dressing over the salad. Any leftover vinaigrette will keep in the fridge for a week.

• Per serving 483 kcalories, protein 18g, carbohydrate 18g, fat 38g, saturated fat 9g, fibre 2g, added sugar none, salt 1.52g

If you like lots of dressing,
simply double the quantities.

Mozzarella and Mango Salad

FOR THE DRESSING
5 tbsp extra virgin olive oil
1 tsp sweet chilli sauce
3 tbsp chopped fresh basil leaves
2 tbsp lemon or lime juice

FOR THE SALAD
2 ripe medium-sized mangoes
3 × 125g balls mozzarella cheese
(preferably buffalo)
100g bag rocket (preferably wild)
12 slices Serrano ham or prosciutto
few small basil leaves, to garnish

Takes 30 minutes • Serves 4

1 To make the dressing, whisk the olive oil, sweet chilli sauce, chopped basil leaves and 1 tablespoon of the lemon or lime juice together with some seasoning (or whizz everything in a small blender). Taste and add more lemon or lime juice or seasoning if you want.

2 For the salad, peel the mangoes and carefully slice off each fleshy side close to the stone. Slice the flesh lengthways into thin strips. Thinly slice the mozzarella.

3 Pile the rocket in the centre of a platter or four individual plates, and arrange the mango, ham and mozzarella slices around the edge. Drizzle with the dressing. Grind some pepper over and scatter with basil.

• Per serving 596 kcalories, protein 31g, carbohydrate 22g, fat 43g, saturated fat 19g, fibre 4g, added sugar none, salt 3.45g

Crisp and tangy, chicory adds a wonderful flavour to salads.
Just pull off the leaves and discard the core.

Cheddar and Chicory Salad

FOR THE DRESSING
5 tbsp olive oil
2 tsp clear honey
1 tbsp wholegrain mustard
2 tbsp lemon juice

FOR THE SALAD
200g/8oz chicory
1 red-skinned apple
85g/3oz walnut pieces
100g/4oz mature cheddar cheese

Takes 20 minutes • Serves 4

1 To make the dressing, put all the ingredients into a small bowl and blend thoroughly with a small whisk or fork. Season to taste and set aside.

2 Separate the chicory leaves and divide between four plates. Cut the apple into quarters, core and thinly slice. Scatter the apple slices over the chicory and sprinkle with the walnuts.

3 Using a vegetable peeler, make cheddar shavings and scatter over each serving. Drizzle the dressing over the salad and finish with a grating of black pepper before serving.

• Per serving 441 kcalories, protein 10g, carbohydrate 9g, fat 38g, saturated fat 9g, fibre 2g, added sugar 2g, salt 0.59g

Buy a thick slice of ham from the deli counter
for a chunky finish.

Peach, Ham and Cheese Salad

1 cos lettuce, trimmed and
roughly torn
1 carton of salad cress, trimmed
2 peaches, stoned and
cut into thin wedges
100g/4oz edam, rind removed
and cut into sticks
100g/4oz thick-sliced ham,
cut into sticks
warm crusty bread, to serve

FOR THE DRESSING
3 tbsp olive oil
1 tbsp white wine vinegar
1 tsp Dijon mustard
2 tbsp mayonnaise
1 tsp clear honey

Takes 25 minutes • Serves 4

1 Toss the lettuce, cress, peaches, cheese
and ham together in a large salad bowl.
2 Whisk together the dressing ingredients
and season to taste.
3 Toss the salad with the dressing just
before serving. Serve with plenty of warm
crusty bread.

• Per serving 286 kcalories, protein 12g, carbohydrate
7g, fat 23g, saturated fat 7g, fibre 3g, added sugar
none, salt 1.63g

An easy salad to put together and it's versatile too.
Try it with prawns instead of chicken.

Pesto Chicken and Potato Salad

500g/1lb 2oz new potatoes,
unpeeled
350g/12oz skinned cooked chicken
(about 3 breasts),
cut into chunks
100g/4oz baby spinach leaves
2 tbsp pesto
juice of 1 small lemon
3 tbsp olive oil

Takes 25 minutes • Serves 4

1 Drop the potatoes into a pan of salted boiling water and boil for 15 minutes. Drain, then return them to the pan and roughly crush with a fork.
2 Tip the chunks of chicken into the pan and scatter in the spinach leaves. Mix gently using a large spoon.
3 Mix the pesto, lemon juice and olive oil, then tip into the pan, season to taste and toss to coat everything in the dressing.

• Per serving 365 kcalories, protein 27g, carbohydrate 21g, fat 20g, saturated fat 5g, fibre 2g, added sugar none, salt 0.39g

Check the back of the salad packet to see what you're buying – the ingredients are listed in descending order with the most leaves first.

Peanut Chicken Salad

finely grated zest and juice of 1 lime
2 tbsp soy sauce
1 tsp clear honey
1 tbsp groundnut oil
2 skinned cooked chicken breasts
120g bag herb salad
⅓ cucumber
handful of roasted peanuts

Takes 20 minutes • Serves 2

1 Stir the lime zest and juice with the soy sauce, honey and groundnut oil. Tear the chicken breasts into bite-sized pieces.
2 Tip the bag of salad on to a platter. Halve the piece of cucumber lengthways, then cut it into thin sticks.
3 Pile the chicken on to the leaves and pour over the dressing. Finish with a thatch of cucumber and a scattering of the peanuts.

• Per serving 360 kcalories, protein 43g, carbohydrate 6g, fat 18g, saturated fat 4.1g, fibre 1.8g, added sugar 2.2g, salt 3.07g

If you want a simple but special dish, try this unusual satay salad.
Only the chicken needs cooking – just barbecue, griddle or grill it.

Satay Chicken Salad

4 skinless boneless chicken breasts
½ cucumber, halved lengthways and sliced
1 small red onion, halved and thinly sliced
140g/5oz beansprouts
handful of fresh coriander leaves
2 tbsp olive oil
1 tbsp lime juice

FOR THE DRESSING
5 tbsp crunchy peanut butter
3 tbsp lime juice
1–2 tbsp Thai red curry paste

Takes 30 minutes • Serves 4

1 Heat a griddle until hot. Season the chicken breasts and cook on the griddle for about 8 minutes on each side, until cooked through and seared in attractive stripes.
2 Meanwhile, toss the cucumber, onion, beansprouts, coriander, olive oil and lime juice together in a shallow salad bowl. Mix the dressing ingredients in a jug, using 1 tablespoon of the curry paste and a little water to give the consistency of single cream. Taste the dressing and whisk in another tablespoon of curry paste if you prefer more of a spicy heat.
3 Slice the griddled chicken diagonally and scatter over the salad. Drizzle some of the dressing over and serve the rest separately.

• Per serving 343 kcalories, protein 40g, carbohydrate 5g, fat 18g, saturated fat 1g, fibre 2g, added sugar none, salt 0.55g

This is a clever way to dress up a packet of salad and the finished result will be on the table in just 20 minutes.

Chicken and Bacon Caesar

4 rindless smoked or unsmoked streaky bacon rashers
255g bag ready-to-eat Caesar salad (which includes croûtons, dressing and parmesan cheese)
1 ripe avocado
2 skinned cooked chicken breasts

Takes 20 minutes • Serves 2

1 Fry the bacon in a frying pan for 2–3 minutes on each side. Remove, then sprinkle the croûtons into the fat in the pan and toss over a medium heat for a minute or two to give them flavour and crisp them up.
2 Divide the leaves between two plates. Halve the avocado and remove the stone. Peel the avocado, cut into chunks and scatter over the leaves. Tear the chicken into pieces and scatter on top. Snap the bacon into chunky pieces over the chicken and top with the croûtons.
3 Drizzle the dressing over the salad and finish with a good dusting of parmesan and a grind of pepper.

• Per serving 530 kcalories, protein 39g, carbohydrate 8g, fat 38g, saturated fat 4g, fibre 4g, added sugar none, salt 1.19g

Stretch two chicken breasts to feed four in this unusual salad
with a tangy dressing.

Warm Thai Noodle Salad

2 large skinless boneless chicken
breasts
175g/6oz dried medium egg noodles
2 good handfuls of greens, such as
Chinese leaf, finely shredded
2 carrots, cut into thin strips
8 spring onions, finely sliced
1 red pepper, seeded and
finely sliced
handful of fresh coriander leaves

FOR THE DRESSING
1 red chilli, seeded and
finely chopped
2 garlic cloves, finely chopped
1 tbsp finely chopped fresh
root ginger
2 tbsp soy sauce
juice of 1 lime
2 tbsp olive oil

Takes 30 minutes • Serves 4

1 Preheat the grill to high. Put the chicken on a baking sheet and grill for 10–12 minutes without turning, until cooked through. Meanwhile, cook the noodles according to the packet instructions. Drain and rinse in cold running water to stop them sticking together.
2 Mix the vegetables in a bowl. Thinly slice the chicken and add to the bowl, along with the noodles and coriander leaves.
3 Mix the dressing ingredients together with 2 tablespoons water, pour over the salad and toss well. Serve immediately.

• Per serving 336 kcalories, protein 24g, carbohydrate 40g, fat 10g, saturated fat 1g, fibre 2g, added sugar none, salt 1.7g

Sesame oil has such a wonderfully pungent flavour, you don't need much to make a lively dressing for this fruity chicken salad.

Oriental Chicken and Papaya Salad

5 tsp sesame oil
2 tbsp lime juice
1 tbsp soy sauce
500g/1lb 2oz skinless boneless chicken breasts, sliced in strips
135g bag rocket, watercress and spinach salad
1 bunch spring onions, finely sliced
½ cucumber, chopped
1 large papaya, peeled, seeded and sliced

Takes 30 minutes • Serves 4

1 Whisk 2 teaspoons of the sesame oil in a small bowl with the lime juice and soy sauce to make the dressing. Set aside for later.
2 Heat the remaining oil in a frying pan or wok. Tip in the chicken strips and stir fry for about 8 minutes until golden and cooked, but still moist. Remove from the heat and let the chicken cool for 2–3 minutes.
3 Tip the salad into a large bowl and scatter over the spring onions, cucumber and papaya. Add the chicken and dressing, and toss everything together gently until all the ingredients are well mixed. Serve while the chicken is still warm.

• Per serving 206 kcalories, protein 32g, carbohydrate 7g, fat 6g, saturated fat 1g, fibre 2g, added sugar none, salt 0.91g

This superhealthy dish is also delicious served hot –
just heat up in the microwave.

No-cook Chicken Couscous

100g/4oz plain couscous
100g/4oz frozen peas
200ml/7fl oz hot chicken or
vegetable stock
200g pack cooked chicken fillets
(preferably flavoured,
e.g. Tikka chicken)
1 large tomato, chopped
1 tbsp olive oil, plus extra to serve
squeeze of lemon juice,
about 1 tsp

Takes 20 minutes • Serves 2

1 Tip the couscous into a heatproof bowl with the peas. Pour over the hot stock, cover with a plate to keep the heat in, and soak for 4 minutes.

2 Tear the chicken into good bite-sized strips, then toss half of it on top of the soaked couscous. Mix in with the chopped tomato, then moisten and flavour with the olive oil and lemon juice. Season to your taste.

3 Divide between two plates and top with the rest of the chicken strips. Drizzle over a little extra olive oil and serve.

• Per serving 315 kcalories, protein 31g, carbohydrate 32g, fat 8g, saturated fat 1g, fibre 3g, added sugar none, salt 0.5g

This quick and healthy supper is great for all the family.
Use chicken instead if you prefer.

Cajun Turkey Salad with Guacamole

2 tbsp sesame seeds
2 tbsp groundnut or sunflower oil
500g pack turkey breast steaks,
cut into strips
1 tbsp Cajun spice seasoning
1 large red pepper, seeded,
quartered and sliced
120g bag herb salad
130g tub guacamole
200g bag tortilla chips

Takes 20–30 minutes • Serves 4

1 Heat a large frying pan or wok, sprinkle in the sesame seeds and toss them over a fairly high heat for about a minute until they're slightly golden. Add the oil to the pan or wok, tip in the turkey, Cajun seasoning and red pepper and stir fry for about 5 minutes until the turkey turns from pink to white.
2 While the turkey's sizzling, divide the herb salad between four plates, then, as soon as the turkey's done, spoon it over the salad, being sure to include all the spicy juices. Top each serving with a spoonful of guacamole, pile tortilla chips on the side of each plate and serve.

• Per serving 524 kcalories, protein 37g, carbohydrate 35g, fat 27g, saturated fat 5g, fibre 5g, added sugar none, salt 1.37g

This speedy beef salad is a great way to use up cooked meat. Alternatively you can buy it from the deli counter in any supermarket.

Beef Tabbouleh

100g/4oz bulghur wheat
6 slices of rare cooked beef
2–3 sprigs of fresh mint
handful of fresh coriander
handful of cherry tomatoes
juice of 1–2 limes
splash of Thai fish sauce

Takes 35 minutes • Serves 2

1 Tip the bulghur wheat into a bowl and pour over hot water to cover. Leave to soak for 30 minutes.

2 Meanwhile, shred the beef. Strip the leaves from the mint sprigs, chop the coriander and halve the tomatoes.

3 To serve, drain the bulghur wheat well and tip into a bowl. Tear in the mint leaves and toss with the beef, coriander, tomatoes, lime juice, fish sauce and seasoning to taste.

• Per serving 440 kcalories, protein 54g, carbohydrate 39g, fat 9g, saturated fat 3.3g, fibre 0.3g, added sugar none, salt 0.56g

Enjoy the different tastes in this easy-to-make main-meal salad.
Halve the quantities for a stunning starter.

Spicy Chorizo and Avocado Salad

4 tbsp olive oil
1 small ciabatta, torn into small
bite-sized pieces
2 × 80g packs sliced chorizo
250g/9oz baby plum or cherry
tomatoes, halved
2 tbsp balsamic vinegar
pinch sugar
1 large ripe avocado, halved,
stoned and sliced
150g bag baby leaf and herb salad

Takes 25 minutes • Serves 4

1 Heat 2 tablespoons of the oil in a large non-stick frying pan. Fry the ciabatta for 8–10 minutes, tossing occasionally, until starting to crisp and brown, then tip into a large salad bowl.
2 Lay the chorizo in the pan and dry fry for 2 minutes until it gives out a red oil. Toss in the tomatoes and cook over a high heat for 1–2 minutes until they start to soften. Drizzle over the vinegar, add the sugar and season.
3 Gently toss the avocado, salad and remaining olive oil with the croûtons. Spoon over the chorizo and tomatoes and drizzle with any pan juices. Serve immediately.

• Per serving 430 kcalories, protein 12g, carbohydrate 26g, fat 31g, saturated fat 7g, fibre 4g, added sugar 1g, salt 1.42g

This is a good-value storecupboard salad that can be enjoyed any day of the week. For a meat-free version use mozzarella instead of prosciutto.

Deli Pasta Salad

300g/10oz farfalle (pasta bows)
200g/8oz frozen peas
1 large tomato, roughly chopped
10 sun-dried tomatoes in oil
2 tbsp olive oil
2 tsp white wine vinegar
1 garlic clove
large handful of fresh basil leaves
85g pack prosciutto or salami

Takes 25 minutes • Serves 4

1 Boil the pasta in salted water for 8 minutes, add the peas, return to the boil and cook for 2 minutes more until tender. Tip into a colander over the sink, cool the pasta and peas under the cold tap, then drain well.
2 While the pasta is boiling, put the tomato in a food processor with half the sun-dried tomatoes, the olive oil, vinegar, garlic and about eight basil leaves. Season, then whizz until smooth. Tip into a large salad bowl.
3 Add the pasta and peas to the dressing, roughly slice the rest of the sun-dried tomatoes and add to the pasta with the remaining basil leaves. Tear in the prosciutto or salami and toss everything together.

• Per serving 426 kcalories, protein 19g, carbohydrate 64g, fat 12g, saturated fat 2g, fibre 6g, added sugar none, salt 1.68g

A light and tasty wintry salad that looks good
and smells even better.

Sizzling Sausage Salad

1 tbsp olive oil
400g pack good quality sausages
1 red onion, roughly chopped
1 heaped tbsp wholegrain mustard
1 tbsp light muscovado sugar
16 cherry tomatoes
2 Little Gem lettuces
1 large avocado
¼ cucumber
1 tbsp red wine vinegar
crusty bread, to serve

Takes 25 minutes • Serves 4

1 Heat the oil in a wok or deep frying pan.
Snip the sausages into quarters into the pan.
Throw in the onion and fry for a minute or
two until brown, stirring occasionally. Spoon
in the mustard and sugar, tip in the tomatoes
and cook for a few minutes more, stirring
until the tomatoes just start to split and the
mixture is coated in the mustard glaze.
2 Separate the lettuces into leaves, peel,
stone and slice the avocado, halve and slice
the cucumber. Mix them together and pile on
to a platter. Spoon the hot sausage mixture
on top.
3 Stir the vinegar and 1 tablespoon water
into the pan, dislodging any sticky bits. Spoon
the pan juices over the salad and serve with
the crusty bread.

• Per serving 394 kcalories, protein 16g, carbohydrate
15g, fat 30g, saturated fat 8g, fibre 3g, added sugar 4g,
salt 2.17g

This is a wonderfully zingy dish that's perfect for
lunch out in the garden.

Pasta Salad with Pesto Prawns

400g/14oz dried short pasta, such
as rigatoni or penne
about 1 tbsp extra virgin olive oil
200g/8oz cooked peeled prawns
5 tbsp (100g/4oz) green pesto
3 tbsp mayonnaise
juice of ½ lemon or lime
3 tbsp chopped fresh parsley,
preferably flatleaf
few basil leaves, shredded with
your fingers, plus extra
for sprinkling
lemon wedges, for squeezing

Takes 35 minutes • Serves 4

1 Cook the pasta according to the packet
instructions until tender. Drain the pasta into
a colander and hold it under cold running
water to cool down quickly.
2 Drain, and tip the pasta into a large bowl.
Toss in 1 tablespoon olive oil to coat
thoroughly (this helps stop the pasta from
sticking together), then add the prawns.
3 Mix the pesto, mayonnaise and lemon or
lime juice with some seasoning. If you need
to slacken the mixture a bit, stir in a little
more olive oil. Pour the pesto dressing over
the pasta and prawns and toss together.
Stir in the parsley and basil, then pile into
your serving dish and serve scattered with
extra shredded basil leaves, plus lemon
wedges for squeezing.

• Per serving 600 kcalories, protein 24g, carbohydrate
78g, fat 24g, saturated fat 2g, fibre 3g, added sugar
none, salt 2g

This fresh and healthy salad uses mainly ingredients you'll already have at home, so it's perfect for when friends turn up at short notice.

Storecupboard Tuna Salad

500g pack salad potatoes, such as Charlotte
4 tbsp olive oil, plus extra for drizzling
1 tbsp lemon juice
½ tsp chilli powder
1 plump garlic clove, finely chopped
410g can cannellini beans, drained and rinsed
1 small red onion or ½ medium one, finely chopped
good handful of parsley, chopped
200g can tuna (any sort), drained
110g bag mixed salad leaves and herbs

Takes 25 minutes • Serves 4

1 Boil the potatoes for about 15 minutes, until tender. Meanwhile, make the dressing. Whisk the oil, lemon juice, chilli powder and garlic in a bowl big enough to take all the salad. Tip in the cannellini beans, onion and parsley.
2 Drain the potatoes and when cool enough to handle cut them in half lengthways.
3 Now gently stir the potatoes into the salad and flake the tuna. Pile on to a bed of salad leaves, drizzled with a little extra olive oil.

• Per serving 308 kcalories, protein 17g, carbohydrate 34g, fat 12g, saturated fat 2g, fibre 5g, added sugar none, salt 0.56g

Fresh tuna has a lovely meaty texture that's even better
when marinated before cooking.

Griddled Tuna with Bean Salad

2 fresh tuna steaks, about
175g/6oz each
1 tbsp olive oil
1 tbsp lemon juice
1 large garlic clove, crushed
1 tbsp chopped rosemary leaves

FOR THE SALAD
410g can cannellini beans, drained
and rinsed
8 cherry tomatoes, quartered
½ small red onion, thinly sliced
50g bag rocket
2 tbsp extra virgin olive oil
1 tbsp lemon juice
1 tsp wholegrain mustard
1 tsp clear honey

Takes 30–40 minutes, plus marinating
• Serves 2

1 Put the tuna in a shallow dish, drizzle over
the oil and lemon juice and scatter over the
garlic and rosemary. Turn the tuna so it's well
coated. Cover and put in the fridge for at
least 30 minutes.
2 Tip the beans into a large bowl. Toss in the
tomatoes, onion and rocket. Put the oil, lemon
juice, mustard, honey and some seasoning
in a screw-top jar. Seal and set aside.
3 Heat a cast iron ridged grill pan or frying
pan until very hot. Cook the tuna on a
moderately high heat for 2 minutes on each
side – don't overcook or it will be dry.
4 Shake the dressing. Pour over the salad
and mix together. Serve the salad with the
tuna on top.

• Per serving 565 kcalories, protein 54g, carbohydrate
30g, fat 26g, saturated fat 5g, fibre 9g, added sugar
2g, salt 0.67g

Double the ingredients to make a light main course for four people.

Chargrilled Courgette and Salmon Salad

4 tbsp fruity olive oil
juice of 1 lemon
2 tsp dried *herbes de Provence*
1 garlic clove, crushed
8 baby courgettes (200g pack),
cut in half lengthways
2 pieces skinless salmon fillet
(total weight about 300g/10oz),
each cut into 3 strips
85g bag herb salad, to serve

FOR THE DRESSING
3 tbsp fruity olive oil
1 tbsp lemon juice
1 tsp wholegrain mustard
2 tbsp chopped fresh tarragon

Takes 30 minutes • Serves 2

1 Measure the dressing ingredients into a screw-top jar, season, then shake to mix. Set aside. Mix the 4 tablespoons olive oil, lemon juice, herbs and garlic in a bowl with some seasoning. Toss the courgette halves in this marinade to coat.
2 Heat a ridged griddle pan until very hot (or a good non-stick frying pan). Sear the courgettes in batches for 2–3 minutes on each side until just softened. Remove and set aside.
3 Toss the strips of salmon into the remaining marinade in the dish, then chargrill for 1–2 minutes on each side until just cooked. Divide the salad leaves between two plates and lay the courgettes and salmon on top. Re-whisk the dressing and drizzle it over everything.

• Per serving 635 kcalories, protein 31g, carbohydrate 5g, fat 55g, saturated fat 9g, fibre 1g, added sugar none, salt 0.27g

A main-meal summer salad that's
perfect for beginner cooks.

Warm Smoked Mackerel Salad

350g/12oz new potatoes
½ × 200g tub crème fraîche
1 tsp horseradish cream
juice of 1 lemon
2 smoked mackerel fillets (about
200g/8oz total weight), skinned
and flaked
85g bag watercress

Takes 30 minutes • Serves 2

1 Cook the potatoes in a large pan of boiling water for 15–20 minutes or until tender.
2 While the potatoes are cooking, mix the crème fraîche in a large bowl with the horseradish cream and lemon juice. Season with freshly ground black pepper (no need for salt as the mackerel is salty).
3 Drain the potatoes, halve and set aside to cool down for a few minutes. Tip into the crème fraîche mix and stir so it coats them and becomes quite runny. Gently toss in the smoked mackerel and watercress. Pile on to two plates and serve while still warm.

• Per serving 646 kcalories, protein 25g, carbohydrate 31g, fat 48g, saturated fat 17g, fibre 2g, added sugar none, salt 2.19g

If you've got a can of anchovies, add them to this fresh and easy salad with the tuna and olives.

Nifty Niçoise

500g/1lb 2oz baby new potatoes
200g can tuna in olive oil
5 tbsp bottled mustard vinaigrette
1 heaped tbsp mayonnaise
4 eggs
250g/9oz runner beans, diagonally sliced
1 crisp lettuce (cos or romaine), separated into leaves
handful of black olives

Takes 40 minutes • Serves 4

1 Steam the potatoes in a steamer for 18 minutes. Drain the oil from the tuna into a bowl and whisk in the vinaigrette and mayonnaise with some seasoning to make a dressing.

2 Lift the top off the steamer and lower the eggs into the water, ensuring they are covered. Scatter the beans over the potatoes, return to the pan, cover and steam for 8 minutes more.

3 Remove the potatoes, beans and eggs. Plunge the eggs into cold water. Stir the potatoes and beans into the dressing. Shell and halve the eggs. Coarsely shred the lettuce into a salad bowl. Tip the potatoes and beans on top, keeping back 2 spoonfuls of dressing. Flake the tuna over, dot with the eggs and olives and drizzle over the reserved dressing.

• Per serving 520 kcalories, protein 25g, carbohydrate 23g, fat 37g, saturated fat 7g, fibre 3g, added sugar none, salt 0.98g

To give this simple dish a twist you could add hardboiled eggs, sliced cooked potato or crispy bacon pieces.

Pick-and-mix Summer Garden Salad

1 head of British garden lettuce such as Webb or butterhead, outer leaves discarded
175g/6oz cheddar cheese
5 spring onions
2 handfuls of radishes
bunch cherry vine-tomatoes
8 slices of your favourite ham
bottle of your favourite dressing

Takes 5 minutes • Serves 4

1 Tear the lettuce into large pieces.
2 Cut the cheese into finger-sized pieces, shred the spring onions into long strips and halve any large radishes.
3 Arrange all the ingredients with the tomatoes and ham in separate piles on a platter and let everyone help themselves.

• Per serving 257 kcalories, protein 22g, carbohydrate 2g, fat 18g, saturated fat 10g, fibre 1g, added sugar none, salt 2g

This is a great dish for serving a crowd as you can easily increase the quantities. It's even better served with pitta bread.

Greek Chicken and Avocado Salad

1.8kg/4lb roasted chicken,
at room temperature
2 ripe avocados
3 tbsp lemon juice, plus extra
for sprinkling
200g pack feta cheese
½ tsp each dried oregano and mint
½ bunch flatleaf parsley
5 tbsp extra virgin olive oil
2 hearts of romaine lettuce,
roughly shredded
4 tomatoes, cut into wedges
3 spring onions, finely sliced
2 tbsp black kalamata olives

Takes 45 minutes • Serves 6

1 Pull the meat from the chicken and shred it roughly. Halve, stone and peel the avocados, cut crosswise into slices and sprinkle with lemon juice. Crumble the feta cheese and toss with the dried oregano and mint. Pick the leaves off the parsley and set aside.
2 Whisk the 3 tablespoons lemon juice with the olive oil and seasoning. In a large bowl, toss the chicken, lettuce, tomatoes and spring onions, then carefully fold through three quarters of the dressing with the avocados.
3 Season, then scatter over the feta, olives and parsley, and drizzle with the rest of the dressing. Sprinkle extra lemon juice on top.

• Per serving 521 kcalories, protein 31g, carbohydrate 5g, fat 42g, saturated fat 12g, fibre 3g, added sugar none, salt 2.05g

A tasty low-fat salad, full of fresh Asian flavours –
let your guests pour the sauce themselves.

Spicy Chicken Salad

7 tbsp Thai fish sauce
2 skinless boneless chicken breasts
4 tbsp lime juice
2 tbsp caster sugar, or more to taste
½ tsp coarsely ground black pepper
1 small and 3 plump red chillies,
seeded and chopped
200g/8oz white cabbage, finely
shredded
2 carrots, finely shredded
1 small onion, finely sliced
2 tbsp each roughly chopped fresh
mint and coriander leaves
3 garlic cloves
3 tbsp rice vinegar
fresh mint and chopped peanuts,
to serve

Takes 40 minutes, plus marinating •
Serves 4

1 Half fill a wok with water. Add 2 tablespoons of fish sauce and bring to the boil. Lower the heat, add the chicken and simmer for 10 minutes, until cooked. Remove the chicken, cool, then shred. Mix 2 more tablespoons of fish sauce in a large bowl with the lime juice, 1 tablespoon of sugar, the pepper, 1 small chopped chilli, the cabbage, carrots, onion, chicken and herbs. Cover and marinate in the fridge for at least 2 hours.
2 For the sauce, pound the garlic, 3 plump chillies and remaining sugar to a paste, using a pestle and mortar. Mix in the remaining fish sauce, the vinegar and 6 tablespoons water. Add more sugar if necessary.
3 Scatter mint leaves on each plate, top with the salad and sprinkle with peanuts. Serve with the sauce.

• Per serving 212 kcalories, protein 22g, carbohydrate 20g, fat 5g, saturated fat 1g, fibre 3g, added sugar 8g, salt 4.98g

You can buy hot or cold cooked chickens for this fresh and zesty salad at the deli counter in most large supermarkets.

Oriental Chicken and Peach Salad

2 × 1.5kg/3lb 5oz or 3 × 1kg/2½lb cooked chickens, preferably free-range
4 large ripe peaches, stoned
200g/8oz mangetout, thinly shredded lengthways
6 spring onions, very finely sliced
4 tbsp chopped fresh coriander
grated zest and juice of 2 limes
2 tbsp clear honey
2 tsp grated fresh root ginger
2 tbsp soy sauce
6 tbsp sunflower oil
1 tbsp toasted sesame oil
herbed couscous, to serve

Takes 25–35 minutes • Serves 8

1 Remove the meat from the chicken, cut into chunky strips and put in a large mixing bowl. Cut the peaches into wedges and reserve any juice. Add the peaches and juice to the chicken with the mangetout, spring onions and coriander.
2 Put the lime zest and juice, honey, ginger and soy sauce into a small bowl and season. Slowly whisk in the sunflower oil until it thickens, then whisk in the sesame oil.
3 Toss the dressing with the salad and serve with herbed couscous.

• Per serving 520 kcalories, protein 49g, carbohydrate 9g, fat 32g, saturated fat 9g, fibre 2g, added sugar 3g, salt 1.05g

Buy a bottle of honey and mustard dressing or mix up your own version.

Chicken Salad with Honey Dressing

450g/1lb new potatoes, scrubbed
and quartered lengthways
175g/6oz fine green beans, trimmed
6 rashers rindless streaky bacon
120g bag mixed salad leaves
4 roasted chicken breasts, skinned
and cut into chunks, or about
700g/1lb 9oz cooked chicken
ready-made honey and
mustard dressing

Takes 40 minutes • Serves 4

1 Cook the potatoes in boiling salted water for 8–10 minutes. Add the beans to the water and cook for a further 3 minutes until just tender. Drain, cool quickly under running cold water, then cool completely.

2 Meanwhile, fry or grill the bacon for 3–4 minutes until crispy. Allow to cool, then break into small pieces.

3 Scatter the salad leaves, potatoes and beans over a large serving plate. Toss the chicken with the dressing to taste, then spoon over the salad leaves. Scatter the crispy bacon over the salad and serve.

• Per serving 505 kcalories, protein 42g, carbohydrate 26g, fat 27g, saturated fat 5g, fibre 3g, added sugar 6g, salt 2.02g

If the weather is fine, cook this zesty chicken dish on the barbecue and keep those cooking smells out of the kitchen.

Sizzling Chicken Platter

4 skinless boneless chicken breasts
1½–2 tsp hot chilli paste or harissa
7 tbsp olive oil
2 tbsp lemon juice
2 ripe vine tomatoes
1–2 lettuces, depending on size, such as cos, Batavia or Webb's
⅓ cucumber, sliced
½ bunch radishes, sliced
25g/1oz pine nuts, toasted
handful of mint leaves

Takes 45 minutes • Serves 4

1 Lay the chicken in a shallow dish. Whisk 1 teaspoon of the chilli paste or harissa, 3 tablespoons of the oil, 1 tablespoon of the lemon juice and a little salt. Pour and rub over the chicken to coat. For the dressing, halve, seed and dice the tomatoes. Mix with ½–1 teaspoon chilli paste and the rest of the lemon juice and oil. Set aside.
2 Heat a griddle, or a barbecue, then cook the chicken for 6–8 minutes on each side until cooked. Remove and keep warm wrapped in foil. Separate the lettuces and spread the leaves on a platter. Scatter over the cucumber and radishes.
3 Cut the chicken into strips and toss with half the dressing. Tip on to the salad and scatter with pine nuts and mint. Drizzle over the remaining dressing and serve.

• Per serving 377 kcalories, protein 32.2g, carbohydrate 4g, fat 26g, saturated fat 3.7g, fibre 1.5g, added sugar none, salt 0.23g

Serve this fabulous new take on a much-loved classic with a bowl of new potatoes.

Jubilee Chicken

600g/1lb 5oz cold cooked chicken (if you are roasting a chicken specially, you will need one that weighs about 1.8kg/4lb, or 5–6 boneless breasts, depending on their size)
350–450g/12oz–1lb cherries
mixed bag rocket, spinach and watercress (or 2 × 85g bags watercress)
bunch spring onions

FOR THE DRESSING
1 tbsp korma curry paste
1 tsp clear honey
1 tbsp lemon juice
200g tub natural low-fat fromage frais
good bunch mint

Takes 25 minutes • Serves 6–8

1 Tear the chicken into bite-sized pieces. Stone the cherries. Tip the curry paste, honey, lemon juice and fromage frais into a food processor or blender with some seasoning. Add the mint leaves stripped from their stalks. Blend until fairly smooth, but with flecks of mint, rather than a purée. Store the dressing in the fridge.
2 Spread the salad leaves or watercress over a platter, scatter over the chicken pieces, then the cherries. Trim both ends off the spring onions, then cut them into long diagonal slices and scatter them over the chicken. (You can now cover the platter with cling film and chill it for up to 2 hours.)
3 Just before serving, drizzle the dressing over the chicken, cherries and leaves.

• Per serving for six 210 kcalories, protein 34g, carbohydrate 9g, fat 4g, saturated fat 1.2g, fibre 0.9g, added sugar 0.6g, salt 0.29g

For a special touch add herbs to the salad dressing – finely snipped chives, fragrant thyme, bruised rosemary sprigs or peppery basil.

Warm Roast Asparagus Salad

500g/1lb 2oz plump asparagus
4 ripe tomatoes, halved
3 tbsp extra virgin olive oil
12 thin rashers streaky bacon
1 tsp clear honey
16 small potatoes, preferably Jersey Royals
2 tbsp red wine vinegar
1 tsp Dijon mustard
100g pack rocket or baby spinach leaves

Takes 45 minutes • Serves 4

1 Preheat the oven to 200°C/Gas 6/fan oven 180°C. Lay the asparagus in a single layer on a baking tray with sides. Nestle the tomatoes in with the asparagus, season and drizzle with 1 tablespoon of the olive oil. Roll each bacon rasher into a tight roll, arrange in the tray and drizzle with honey. Bake for 20 minutes until the tomatoes are soft and the bacon is crisp.
2 Meanwhile, boil the potatoes until tender. Whisk the vinegar, remaining olive oil, the mustard and some seasoning in a large bowl until blended. Toss the leaves in half the dressing and arrange on a serving platter.
3 Drain the potatoes and cut in half. Gently toss them in the remaining dressing, arrange on the platter with the asparagus and tuck in the tomatoes and bacon.

• Per serving 295 kcalories, protein 13g, carbohydrate 22g, fat 18g, saturated fat 4g, fibre 4g, added sugar 1g, salt 1.43g

You can make the dressing for this low-fat dish the day before and cook the pork a couple of hours before serving.

Vietnamese Pork Salad

1 tsp golden caster sugar
grated zest of and juice of 2 limes
2 fresh red chillies, seeded and finely chopped
handful of coriander stems, chopped
1 tbsp each sesame oil, Thai fish sauce and light soy sauce
50g/2oz sesame seeds, dry roasted
500g/1lb 2oz pork tenderloin, trimmed of fat
vegetable oil, for brushing
¼ white cabbage, shredded
1 cucumber, cut into matchsticks
5 celery sticks, cut into matchsticks
3 spring onions, finely sliced
2 trimmed lemongrass stalks, finely sliced
handful each of coriander and mint leaves, chopped

Takes 1 hour 10 minutes • Serves 6

1 To make the dressing, put the sugar and lime juice in a pan with 1 tablespoon water. Heat to dissolve the sugar. Add 1 of the chillies and the coriander stems, then pulse in a blender until smooth. Tip into a bowl and stir in the sesame oil, fish sauce, soy sauce and sesame seeds.

2 Preheat the oven to 200°C/Gas 6/fan oven 180°C and heat a griddle pan. Brush the pork with oil and griddle for a few minutes until seared. Put on a baking sheet and roast for 10–12 minutes until cooked. Cool, then thinly slice. Tip into a bowl and pour over half the dressing.

3 Toss the remaining ingredients in a bowl with the remaining dressing, chilli and lime zest. Pile on to a platter, top with the pork and spoon over any juices.

• Per serving 195 kcalories, protein 21g, carbohydrate 4g, fat 11g, saturated fat 2g, fibre 2g, added sugar 1g, salt 1.1g

The dressing is made by mixing vinaigrette and olive tapenade for a summery Provençal flavour. Serve with buttered new potoates.

Rare Tapenade Beef Salad

800–900g/1¾lb beef roasting joint, such as fillet, topside or sirloin
olive oil, for brushing
2 heads chicory, leaves separated
6 spring onions, trimmed and shredded
100g bag rocket
20g pack fresh flatleaf parsley, stalks removed
125ml/4fl oz vinaigrette dressing, preferably homemade
1 bunch radishes, quartered
3 tbsp olive tapenade
about 18 large caper berries (with stalks)

Takes 1 hour • Serves 6

1 Preheat the oven to 200°C/Gas 6/fan oven 180°C. Brush the beef lightly with oil in a small roasting tin and season. Roast for 20 minutes. Baste with any juices and reduce the heat to 180°C/Gas 4/fan oven 160°C. Roast for another 20 minutes for rare, 30 minutes for medium-rare. Remove and cool to room temperature.

2 Lay the chicory leaves around the edge of a platter. Mix the spring onions with the rocket and parsley leaves in a large bowl.

3 Thinly carve the beef and season. Mix any meat juices into half the vinaigrette and toss with the rocket mixture. Spoon this on to the centre of the platter, scatter with the radishes and arrange the meat on top. Mix the tapenade into the remaining vinaigrette, spoon over the salad and garnish with caper berries.

• Per serving 407 kcalories, protein 29g, carbohydrate 3g, fat 31g, saturated fat 7.6g, fibre 1.3g, added sugar 0.2g, salt 1.17g

This piquant salad is eaten as lettuce parcels, with the ingredients served in bowls so everyone can help themselves.

Waterfall Beef Salad

2 thick-cut sirloin steaks
(600g/1lb 5oz in total)
4 tbsp lime juice (about 2–3 limes)
2 tbsp Thai fish sauce
1 tbsp light muscovado sugar
1 red chilli, seeded and thinly sliced
2 tbsp chopped mint leaves
4 spring onions, chopped

TO SERVE
iceberg, Romaine or Webb's lettuce
few sprigs of mint
100g/4oz beansprouts
1 bunch radishes, thinly sliced
2–3 large carrots, cut into
thin matchsticks

Takes 25 minutes • Serves 4

1 Grill the steaks for 2–3 minutes on each side until medium-rare. When cool, slice thinly.
2 Mix the lime juice, fish sauce, sugar, chilli, mint and spring onions. Toss in the beef and tip into a serving bowl.
3 To serve, arrange the remaining ingredients in bowls, so everyone can help themselves to lettuce, etc., to wrap around the beef.

• Per serving 369 kcalories, protein 38g, carbohydrate 14g, fat 18g, saturated fat 8g, fibre 3g, added sugar 4g, salt 1.63g

Serve with a bottle of olive oil for drizzling and
a bottle of Italian wine.

Italian Antipasti Platter

8 small tomatoes
5 tbsp mayonnaise
1 tsp capers
3 canned anchovy fillets,
drained and chopped
80g can tuna, drained
3 tbsp basil or olive oil
1 tbsp lemon juice
handful of fresh basil, shredded
1 garlic clove, finely chopped
1 large avocado, stoned and peeled
8 very thin slices of ham

TO SERVE
175g/6oz dolcelatte cheese
a selection of Italian breads, olives,
meats and sun-dried and
marinated vegetables
(such as peppers, tomatoes,
courgettes, artichokes)

Takes 35 minutes • Serves 4

1 Cut a thin slice off the top of each tomato and scoop out and discard the seeds. Mix the mayonnaise, capers and anchovies. Flake and gently stir in the tuna. Season if necessary. Spoon the filling into the tomatoes.
2 Make the dressing. Mix the oil, lemon juice, basil, garlic and seasoning. Slice the avocado into eight wedges and wrap the ham loosely around each wedge.
3 To serve, lay everything out, including the cheese, etc., on one large or two small platters. Drizzle the dressing over the avocado wedges.

• Per serving 371 kcalories, protein 12g, carbohydrate 3g, fat 34g, saturated fat 5.3g, fibre 2.1g, added sugar none, salt 1.28g

Pile this colourful, crunchy meal on to a platter,
then grab your chopsticks and dig in.

Thai Prawn Platter

finely grated zest of 1 and
juice of 2 limes
2 tbsp sunflower oil
2 tsp Thai fish sauce
1 garlic clove, finely chopped
4 tsp golden caster sugar
250g/9oz cooked tiger prawns
1 bunch each radishes and
spring onions
2–3 celery sticks
300g/10oz combination of baby
carrots, baby corn and
sugar snap peas
140g/5oz fresh beansprouts
1 lettuce, such as Webb's
25g/1oz roasted salted peanuts,
chopped

Takes 35 minutes • Serves 4

1 Mix the lime zest and juice (about 4 tablespoons) with the oil, fish sauce, garlic and sugar for the dressing. Peel the prawns, leaving the tails on. Tip them into a bowl and pour in one third of the dressing. Set aside.

2 Thinly slice the radishes, spring onions and celery, then thinly slice the carrots and corn lengthways and halve the sugar snap peas lengthways. Toss together with the beansprouts, prawns and remaining dressing. Season if necessary.

3 Lay a bed of lettuce leaves on a large platter and spoon the salad on top. Sprinkle with peanuts and serve.

• Per serving 222 kcalories, protein 20g, carbohydrate 13g, fat 10g, saturated fat 1.5g, fibre 3.6g, added sugar 5.3g, salt 3.2g

You can easily double the quantities if you are feeding a crowd and much of this sensational salad can be prepared several hours ahead.

Salmon and Crisp Prosciutto Salad

4 salmon fillets, about 500g/1lb 2oz total weight
500g/1lb 2oz new potatoes, halved
4 tbsp mayonnaise
1 tbsp tarragon vinegar
1 tbsp chopped fresh tarragon
4 tbsp olive oil
pinch sugar
6 slices prosciutto
2 × 90g bags watercress and spinach salad, or 1 bunch watercress and 2 Little Gem lettuces
1 bunch spring onions, sliced
2 tbsp drained capers

Takes 45 minutes • Serves 4

1 Lay the salmon in a microwave-proof dish, season, then microwave on high (lightly covered) for 5–6 minutes, until the flesh flakes. Leave to cool.
2 Cook the potatoes in a pan of boiling water for 10–15 minutes, until tender. Drain. Make the dressing – whisk the mayonnaise, vinegar, tarragon, 3 tablespoons of the oil and the sugar. Season. Heat the remaining oil in a frying pan. Cut each slice of prosciutto into three and fry quickly until crisp. Drain on kitchen paper.
3 Lay the salad leaves on a platter. Break the salmon into chunks, then put in a bowl with the warm potatoes and half the spring onions and capers. Mix in the dressing. Pile on to the salad leaves, scatter with the prosciutto and remaining spring onions and capers.

• Per serving 600 kcalories, protein 36.1g, carbohydrate 23g, fat 41.2g, saturated fat 7.8g, fibre 2.7g, added sugar 0.5g, salt 1.84g

Forget knives and forks – it's much more fun to eat this feast with your fingers. And adults can wash it down with a cold beer.

Indian Feast

250g tub natural yogurt
15g pack coriander, finely chopped
1 plump green chilli, seeded and finely chopped
1 tsp clear honey
1 small red onion
1 medium mango, peeled and chopped
7 tbsp olive oil
2 lemons
pinch dried chilli flakes
2 × 410g cans chickpeas, drained and rinsed
2 garlic cloves, chopped

TO SERVE
bought Indian snacks, such as samosas and bhajias, 8 chapatis (warmed), 2 Little Gem lettuces and ½ cucumber, cut into sticks

Takes 35 minutes • Serves 4

1 Mix the yogurt, coriander, chilli and honey for the raita. Finely chop half the red onion; thinly slice the rest. For the salsa, combine the chopped onion with the mango, 1 tablespoon of the oil, a squeeze of juice from 1 of the lemons and the chilli flakes.
2 Whizz the chickpeas with the remaining oil, the garlic, 4 tablespoons of the raita, a squeeze of lemon juice and seasoning in a blender.
3 Warm up the Indian snacks. Lay a lettuce leaf in the centre of each chapati, spoon on some chickpea mix, then fold the chapatis to make wraps, tucking in some of the onion slices. Cut the remaining lemon into wedges. Arrange with the snacks and wraps on a platter with the rest of the lettuce leaves and raita, the cucumber and salsa.

• Per serving 405 kcalories, protein 13g, carbohydrate 37g, fat 24g, saturated fat 3.1g, fibre 7.3g, added sugar 1g, salt 0.82g

Diced oven chips create brilliant hot potato croûtons and make the salad more substantial.

Chilli Chicken and Bacon Salad

2 boneless skinless chicken breast fillets
2½ tbsp sweet chilli dipping sauce
2 tbsp lime juice
175g/6oz oven chips
5 rashers streaky bacon
½ × 75g bag watercress
2 heads chicory, thickly sliced
4 spring onions, trimmed and sliced at an angle
2 small avocados, peeled, stoned and cut into wedges

Takes 25–35 minutes • Serves 2

1 Preheat the oven to 220°C/Gas 7/fan oven 200°C. Brush both sides of the chicken with ½ tablespoon chilli sauce, season well and put on a large baking tray. Mix 2 tablespoons chilli sauce with the lime juice and 1 tablespoon water to make a dressing.

2 Dice the oven chips and scatter round the chicken on the baking tray, then add the bacon rashers. Bake in the oven for 15 minutes until the potatoes and bacon are crispy and the chicken is cooked, but still nice and juicy.

3 Toss the watercress, chicory, spring onions and avocados in half the dressing and pile on to a platter. Slice the chicken and scatter on top of the salad with the bacon and potato. Spoon over the remaining dressing and eat while it's still warm.

• Per serving 676 kcalories, protein 48g, carbohydrate 39g, fat 38g, saturated fat 7g, fibre 7g, added sugar 7g, salt 2.47g

Halloumi is a classic Cypriot cheese flavoured with mint.
When cooked, it gets soft and squidgy but still holds its shape.

Summer Couscous Salad

250g/9oz couscous
250ml/9fl oz hot vegetable stock
400g can chickpeas,
drained and rinsed
1–2 tbsp vegetable or olive oil
300g/10oz courgettes, sliced
300g/10oz small vine-ripened
tomatoes, halved
250g pack halloumi cheese,
thickly sliced
and halved lengthways

FOR THE DRESSING
125ml/4fl oz olive oil
3 tbsp lime juice
2 large garlic cloves, finely chopped
2 tbsp chopped fresh mint
½ tsp sugar

Takes 35 minutes • Serves 4

1 Tip the couscous into a bowl, pour the stock over and stir. Cover and leave for 4 minutes. Tip all the dressing ingredients into a bowl and mix. Fluff up the couscous with a fork, then mix in the chickpeas and half the dressing. Pile on to a platter.

2 Heat 1 tablespoon oil in a large frying pan and fry the courgette slices over a high heat for 2–3 minutes until dark golden. Drain on kitchen paper. Cook the tomatoes, cut-side down in the pan, for 2 minutes until tinged brown. Top the couscous with the courgettes and tomatoes.

3 Fry the halloumi strips in the pan, with more oil if needed, for 2–3 minutes, turning, until crisp and brown. Pile on top of the tomatoes, and drizzle with the remaining dressing.

• Per serving 721 kcalories, protein 23g, carbohydrate 47g, fat 50g, saturated fat 14g, fibre 4g, added sugar 1g, salt 2.86g

This delicious salad makes the perfect
light summer lunch.

Spinach and Feta Salad

250g/9oz couscous
300ml/½ pint hot vegetable stock
300g/10oz frozen broad beans
125g bag baby spinach leaves
20g pack fresh mint
85g/3oz black olives
200g pack feta cheese
olive oil, for drizzling

Takes 25 minutes • Serves 4

1 Put the couscous in a large bowl, pour over the boiling stock and stir. Cover and leave for 4 minutes. Cook the broad beans in boiling water for 3 minutes, then drain. Fluff up the couscous with a fork.

2 Tip the spinach into a colander and pour boiling water over to wilt it. Refresh under cold water and squeeze dry.

3 Pick the leaves from the mint stems and chop them. Stir the broad beans, spinach, mint and olives into the couscous. Crumble in the feta, season to taste and drizzle with plenty of olive oil. Toss well and serve.

• Per serving 410 kcalories, protein 17g, carbohydrate 39g, fat 22g, saturated fat 8g, fibre 6g, added sugar none, salt 3.16g

Use the same quantities for a starter for 6–8 people, maybe followed by some barbecued vegetables, or meats for non-vegetarians.

Goat's Cheese Croûton Salad

2 red peppers, quartered and seeded
1 thin baguette, cut into 16 slices
2 tbsp olive oil
200g/8oz firm goat's cheese, cut into 16 slices
handful of black olives, halved and stoned
large bunch flat leaf parsley, chopped
½ red onion, finely chopped
large bag mixed salad leaves, with frisée, radicchio and red chicory

FOR THE DRESSING
6 tbsp olive oil
2 tbsp walnut oil
2 tsp Dijon mustard
4 tbsp white wine vinegar

Takes 40 minutes • Serves 4

1 Grill the peppers, skin-side up, until the skins are blackened. Cover with foil until cool, then strip off the skins. Slice the peppers in strips and put in a bowl. Preheat the oven to 200°C/Gas 6/fan oven 180°C.
2 Lay the baguette slices on a baking sheet. Brush with oil. Put a slice of goat's cheese on each piece of bread and bake for 10 minutes until the bread is crisp. Meanwhile, add the olives, parsley and onion to the peppers. Put the dressing ingredients in a screw-top jar with some seasoning and shake well.
3 Toss the salad leaves and the red pepper mixture with three quarters of the dressing and place on a platter. Tuck the toasts among the leaves and drizzle with the rest of the dressing.

• Per serving 651 kcalories, protein 19.3g, carbohydrate 48g, fat 43.6g, saturated fat 12.9g, fibre 3.2g, added sugar none, salt 2.47g

Soft, rindless goat's cheeses come in a variety of shapes and are often coated in herbs or pepper. Use a mild one for this dish.

No-cook Salad Pizza

1 round focaccia loaf or
long ciabatta
200g tub marinated grilled red and
yellow peppers in olive oil
3 tbsp pesto
85g bag watercress
100g/4oz soft goat's cheese
handful of black olives

Takes 10 minutes • Serves 4–6

1 Slice the bread in half so you have two round or long bases. Drain the peppers, reserving the oil.

2 Spread 1 tablespoon of the pesto over the cut side of each base. Scatter over the peppers and watercress and crumble over the goat's cheese.

3 Mix the remaining tablespoon of pesto with a tablespoon of oil from the peppers and drizzle it over the pizzas. Scatter the olives over. Cut each pizza into wedges or slices and serve.

• Per serving for four 388 kcalories, protein 13g, carbohydrate 34g, fat 22g, saturated fat 5.6g, fibre 2.2g, added sugar 1.1g, salt 2.57g

Get creative with this healthy
and unusual salad.

Beetroot, Feta and Asparagus Salad

FOR THE DRESSING
large handful of fresh oregano or
marjoram leaves
1 garlic clove
juice of 1½ lemons
4 tbsp extra virgin olive oil

FOR THE SALAD
250g/9oz bunch asparagus, cut
into 3cm/1¼in lengths
2 × 250g packs boiled fresh
beetroot, cut into quarters
grated zest of 1 lemon
2 spring onions, finely sliced
85g bag watercress, large
stalks removed
20 basil leaves, green or purple,
or both
400g/14oz feta or goat's cheese

Takes 30 minutes • Serves 6

1 Pulse the oregano or marjoram, a pinch of salt and the garlic to a paste in a food processor for the dressing. Add the lemon juice and whizz until smooth. Stir in the olive oil and season.

2 Cook the asparagus in boiling salted water for 3 minutes. Drain and cool under the cold tap.

3 Put the beetroot in a large bowl and toss with two thirds of the dressing, the lemon zest, spring onions and watercress. Tear in the basil. Toss in the asparagus and season with black pepper. Taste before adding salt as the cheese is quite salty. Mix lightly, so you don't dye everything pink, then pile into a serving dish. Crumble over the cheese and pour over the remaining dressing.

• Per serving 286 kcalories, protein 14g, carbohydrate 10g, fat 21g, saturated fat 9g, fibre 2g, added sugar none, salt 3.02g

Use less salty Lancashire cheese in place
of feta, if you prefer.

Two-cheese Salad with Croûtons

2 thick slices white bread,
crusts removed
1 tsp paprika
2 tbsp olive oil
1 garlic clove, crushed
1 large cos or romaine lettuce
2 ripe avocados
2 tbsp lemon juice
1 large courgette, cut into sticks
140g/5oz feta cheese, crumbled
into chunks
25g/1oz parmesan cheese,
finely grated
6 tbsp olive oil dressing
(ready-made)

Takes 30 minutes • Serves 4

1 Preheat the oven to 220°C/Gas 7/fan
oven 200°C. Cut the bread into 2cm/¾in
cubes. Toss with the paprika, olive oil and
garlic, then spread out on a baking sheet.
Bake for 7–8 minutes, until crisp.
2 Tear the lettuce into large pieces. Peel,
stone and slice the avocados and toss with
the lemon juice and freshly ground black
pepper.
3 Mix the lettuce, courgette, feta cheese
and croûtons. Put into a large salad bowl
with the avocado and sprinkle with the
parmesan. Drizzle olive oil dressing over
the salad to serve.

• Per serving 453 kcalories, protein 12g, carbohydrate
12g, fat 40g, saturated fat 10g, fibre 4g, added sugar
none, salt 1.92g

A simple yet substantial salad,
with a minimum of preparation.

New Potato and Pepper Salad

450g/1lb new potatoes, halved
6 tbsp olive oil
juice of ½ lemon
1 tbsp wholegrain mustard
2 × 150g balls mozzarella cheese, drained and torn
180g bag baby leaf spinach
200g tub roasted peppers in olive oil, drained and torn
handful of fresh basil

Takes 20 minutes • Serves 4

1 Cook the potatoes in boiling water for 10–15 minutes, then drain.
2 Make the dressing by whisking together the oil, lemon juice, mustard and some seasoning.
3 Put all the other ingredients, including the warm potatoes, in a large bowl. Drizzle over the dressing and lightly toss. Serve immediately.

• Per serving 517 kcalories, protein 23g, carbohydrate 22g, fat 38g, saturated fat 13g, fibre 3g, added sugar none, salt 2.09g

A main-course salad that's good value too.
Vary the ingredients according to what you've got in your fridge.

Winter Crunch Salad

1 × 170g ready-to-bake garlic bread
2 heads chicory
2 celery sticks, cut into thin diagonal slices
1 bunch radishes, trimmed and quartered
50g/2oz shelled walnuts or pecans, toasted and roughly chopped
2 red-skinned eating apples, cored and cut into slim wedges
175g/6oz stilton cheese
4–5 tbsp ready-made honey and mustard dressing, to serve

Takes 20 minutes • Serves 4

1 Preheat the oven and cook the garlic bread according to the packet instructions.
2 Separate the chicory into leaves and toss in a large bowl with the celery, radishes, nuts and apples. Crumble the stilton in large chunks over the top.
3 Cut half the garlic bread into the marked slices. Cut the remainder into chunks and toss into the salad with as much dressing as you like. Serve with the remaining garlic bread on the side.

• Per serving 464 kcalories, protein 16g, carbohydrate 29g, fat 32g, saturated fat 10.7g, fibre 2.5g, added sugar none, salt 1.61g

Pulses are an especially useful source of fibre and protein and are great for diabetics, as they allow a steady release of glucose.

Herbed Chickpea Salad

200g/8oz bulghur wheat
50g/2oz pine nuts
1 leek, finely diced
3 tbsp extra virgin olive oil
juice of 2 large lemons
50g/2oz raisins
400g can chickpeas, drained and rinsed
4 tbsp chopped fresh herbs, such as parsley, coriander and/or chives

TO SERVE
iceberg lettuce leaves
strips of red pepper
radishes
celery sticks

Takes 30 minutes • Serves 6

1 Cook the bulghur wheat according to the packet instructions. Allow to cool. Lightly toast the pine nuts in a non-stick pan over a low heat, until golden.

2 Put all the salad ingredients into a bowl and toss together well. Taste and adjust the seasoning if necessary.

3 Serve piled on to plates or into bowls with iceberg lettuce, red pepper, radishes and celery.

• Per serving 300 kcalories, protein 8g, carbohydrate 39g, fat 13g, saturated fat 2g, fibre 3g, added sugar none, salt 0.25g

Enjoy the delicious flavours of
this healthy vegan salad.

Butter Bean and Tomato Salad

420g can butter beans, drained
and rinsed
500g/1lb 2oz cherry tomatoes,
quartered
2 small green or yellow courgettes
(about 300g/10oz in total),
chopped into small dice
1 small red onion, chopped
15–20g pack fresh coriander,
chopped
2 tbsp lemon juice
3 tbsp olive oil
1 tsp ground cumin

Takes 15 minutes • Serves 6

1 Tip all the ingredients into a bowl with some
seasoning and mix well.
2 Cover and leave at room temperature until
ready to serve. (This salad can happily be
made the day before and chilled.)
3 Bring the salad to room temperature (if it
has been chilled), and give it a good stir
before serving.

• Per serving 109 kcalories, protein 4g, carbohydrate
9g, fat 6g, saturated fat 1g, fibre 3g, added sugar
none, salt 0.41g

Mix and match with other canned beans,
such as butter or flageolet.

Warm Chickpea Salad

1 red onion, cut into wedges
2 courgettes, thickly sliced
1 red pepper, seeded and cut into
large chunks
375g/13oz ripe tomatoes, halved
5 tbsp olive oil
juice of ½ lemon
3 tbsp chopped fresh mixed herbs
(such as chives, parsley and mint)
or 3 tbsp parsley
2 × 400g cans chickpeas or flageolet
beans, drained and rinsed
100g/4oz feta cheese, cut into cubes

Takes 45 minutes • Serves 4

1 Preheat the oven to 220°C/Gas 7/fan oven 200°C. Put the onion, courgettes, pepper and tomatoes in a shallow roasting tin and season with black pepper. Drizzle with 2 tablespoons of the olive oil and toss well. Roast for 30 minutes, stirring halfway through, until the vegetables are cooked and beginning to turn brown.
2 Meanwhile, mix the lemon juice and remaining olive oil to make a dressing. Season and stir in the herbs.
3 When the vegetables are cooked, allow them to cool for 5 minutes, then tip into a bowl with the chickpeas or beans, feta and dressing. Toss lightly before serving. Leftovers are delicious cold, served with pitta bread.

• Per serving 371 kcalories, protein 15g, carbohydrate 28g, fat 23g, saturated fat 5g, fibre 7g, added sugar none, salt 1.62g

Serve with pitta bread for
a delicious picnic dish.

Spiced Two-bean Salad

250g/9oz sugarsnap peas
400g can butter beans
400g can cannellini beans
2 tbsp each olive oil and lemon juice
1 tsp ground cumin
3 tomatoes, cut into eighths
10 medium radishes, finely sliced
6 spring onions, sliced diagonally
handful of fresh mint leaves

FOR THE DRESSING
225ml/8fl oz low-fat yogurt
2 tbsp lemon juice
1 tbsp olive oil
1 garlic clove, crushed

Takes 30 minutes • Serves 6

1 Cook the sugarsnap peas in boiling water for 2 minutes, drain into a sieve, then refresh under cold water. Drain all the beans in a sieve and rinse under the cold tap. Now drain both sugarsnaps and beans really well.
2 Whisk the 2 tablespoons olive oil, lemon juice and the cumin in a large bowl and season. Tip in the sugarsnaps and beans, tomatoes, radishes, spring onions and the mint.
3 Whisk all the dressing ingredients in another bowl with some seasoning. The salad and dressing can be made 24 hours ahead. Keep in the fridge, in separate bowls. Toss the salad and dressing together just before serving.

• Per serving 174 kcalories, protein 10g, carbohydrate 19g, fat 7g, saturated fat 1g, fibre 5g, added sugar none, salt 0.59g

Swap the mozzarella for blue cheese and the basil for chives for a totally different taste.

Warm Mediterranean New Potato Salad

1 tbsp olive oil
2 garlic cloves
500g bag baby new potatoes
500ml/18fl oz hot vegetable stock
125g ball mozzarella cheese,
torn into bite-sized pieces
500g pack cherry tomatoes, halved
50g/2oz pine nuts, toasted
handful of basil leaves, sliced
lettuce leaves, to serve

Takes 30 minutes • Serves 2

1 Heat the oil in a large frying pan and fry the garlic and potatoes for 1–2 minutes. Pour over the stock and simmer, uncovered, for 20 minutes or until the potatoes are cooked. Turn the heat up and let the stock reduce to about 2 tablespoons of sticky glaze.
2 Throw in the mozzarella, tomatoes, pine nuts and basil and give it a stir. When the cheese starts to melt, remove the pan from the heat and share between two plates. Serve with crisp lettuce leaves on the side.

• Per serving 615 kcalories, protein 23g, carbohydrate 50g, fat 37g, saturated fat 11g, fibre 6g, added sugar none, salt 1.6g

This easy, versatile salad will be on the table in less than half an hour.

Minty Rice Salad

250g/9oz long-grain rice
250g bunch asparagus,
cut in bite-sized pieces
1 red pepper, seeded and chopped
3 tbsp olive oil
grated zest and juice 1 lemon
2 × 125g packs mini balls
mozzarella cheese, halved
(or 2 × 125g balls mozzarella
cheese, chopped)
1 large bunch mint leaves, shredded

Takes 25 minutes • Serves 4

1 Drop the rice into a pan of boiling salted water and cook for 10 minutes.
2 Toss in the asparagus and cook for a further 3–4 minutes until the rice is completely cooked and the asparagus is only slightly crunchy. Drain into a sieve and hold under the tap until cool.
3 When the rice is cold, stir in the red pepper, oil, lemon zest and juice, mozzarella and mint leaves. Season and serve.

• Per serving 506 kcalories, protein 22g, carbohydrate 58g, fat 23g, saturated fat 10g, fibre 1g, added sugar none, salt 0.98g

If you can't find bulghar wheat, you can use couscous instead. Just follow the cooking instructions on the packet and continue with step 2.

Spiced Bulghar and Squash Salad

1 butternut squash, about 1kg/2lb 4oz peeled, seeded and cut into small chunks
2 red peppers, seeded and roughly sliced
2 tbsp harissa paste
1 tbsp oil
140g/5oz bulghar wheat
600ml/1 pint hot vegetable stock
1 garlic clove, crushed
juice of ½ lemon
150g carton natural bio-yogurt
400g can chickpeas, drained and rinsed
180g bag baby leaf spinach

Takes 30–40 minutes • Serves 4

1 Heat the oven to 200°C/Gas 6/fan oven 180°C. Toss the squash and red pepper in the harissa paste and oil. Spread the chunks out on a large baking tray and roast for 20 minutes until softened and the edges of the vegetables are starting to char.
2 Meanwhile, put the bulghar wheat in a large bowl and pour over the hot stock. Cover tightly with cling film and leave for 15 minutes until the grains are tender but still have a little bite. In a separate bowl, mix the garlic and lemon juice into the yogurt and season.
3 Let the bulghar wheat cool slightly, then toss in the roasted vegetables, chickpeas and spinach – the leaves may wilt a little. Season, if you want, drizzle with the garlicky yogurt and serve warm.

• Per serving 388 kcalories, protein 15g, carbohydrate 66g, fat 9g, saturated fat 1g, fibre 9g, added sugar none, salt 1.18g

This dish is a wonderful, quick-as-a-flash way of using up leftover vegetables, as you use a food processor for the slicing and grating.

Boxing Day Salad

½ red cabbage, about 450g/1lb
2 celery sticks, with their leaves
175g/6oz fresh Brussels sprouts, trimmed
1 red-skinned eating apple, cored, but with the skin left on
2 carrots, peeled
175g/6oz mixed nuts, such as brazils, walnuts and roasted cashews
100g/4oz stilton cheese

FOR THE DRESSING
6 tbsp light olive or sunflower oil
4 tbsp cranberry sauce
5 tbsp fresh orange juice

Takes 15 minutes • Serves 4–6

1 Cut the hard white core from the cabbage, then shred the leaves and slice the celery, sprouts and apple in a food processor. With the grating attachment, grate the carrots. Roughly chop the nuts, either in the processor or by hand.
2 In a small bowl, mix the oil with the cranberry sauce. It will look quite cloudy and thick, but add the orange juice next and it will all thin out into a fruity dressing.
3 Tip all the chopped vegetables and nuts into a big bowl, pour in the dressing and toss together. (The salad will keep in a covered container for up to a day in the fridge.) Season and serve with stilton crumbled over the top.

• Per serving for four 620 kcalories, protein 19g, carbohydrate 25g, fat 50g, saturated fat 11.6g, fibre 9.1g, added sugar 3.3g, salt 0.92g

The toasted pumpkin seeds add a surprise crunch
to this sharp, sweet salad.

Exotic Avocado Salad

3 tbsp pumpkin seeds
2 ripe papayas
3 ripe avocados
85g bag trimmed and washed watercress
20g pack fresh mint
juice of 1 lime
3 tbsp olive oil

Takes 20 minutes • Serves 6

1 Dry fry the pumpkin seeds in a frying pan for a few minutes, tossing them until toasted. Tip them out of the pan and cool. Peel the papayas, halve them lengthways and scoop out the seeds. Cut the flesh into long, thin slices. Stone the avocados, then peel and slice the flesh lengthways into thin slices.
2 Put the papayas, avocados, pumpkin seeds and watercress into a large bowl. Chop about 1 tablespoon of the mint leaves and set aside. Pick the remaining leaves from the stalks and tear them into the bowl.
3 Mix the lime juice and olive oil with the reserved chopped mint and season. Pour over the salad and gently mix everything together with your hands. Transfer to a serving platter.

• Per serving 260 kcalories, protein 4g, carbohydrate 11g, fat 22g, saturated fat 3g, fibre 5g, added sugar none, salt 0.05g

You can find avocado oil in most supermarkets – it's very good for you as it's low in saturated fat and contains no cholesterol.

Dressed Little Gems

4 tbsp avocado oil or olive oil
1 tbsp balsamic vinegar,
white or dark
4 Little Gem lettuces,
cut into wedges
50g/2oz parmesan cheese shavings

Takes 10 minutes • Serves 8

1 Mix the oil and vinegar with a generous pinch of salt (preferably flakes) to make the dressing.
2 Arrange the lettuce on a platter.
3 Drizzle with the dressing and scatter with the parmesan shavings.

• Per serving 84 kcalories, protein 3g, carbohydrate 1g, fat 8g, saturated fat 2g, fibre none, added sugar none, salt 0.42g

Use a good-quality pesto – it will make all the difference.
You can add different coloured lettuce leaves to the rocket for variety.

Asparagus Salad with Pesto Dressing

200g/8oz small new potatoes, unpeeled
500g/1lb 2oz asparagus
50g/2oz rocket leaves
3 tbsp pesto
2 tbsp olive oil
2 tsp lemon juice
25g/1oz parmesan cheese shavings

Takes 20 minutes • Serves 6–8

1 Thinly slice the potatoes and boil until just tender, about 3–4 minutes. Drain and leave to cool. Snap the asparagus spears where they break naturally and discard the tough ends.

2 Bring a wide, shallow pan of salted water to the boil and cook the asparagus until just tender, about 3–4 minutes. Drain and cool under running water.

3 Divide the rocket leaves between six side plates. Scatter the potato slices over, then arrange the asparagus on top. Mix together the pesto, oil and lemon juice, add seasoning to taste and drizzle over. Scatter with parmesan shavings.

• Per serving for six 122 kcalories, protein 6g, carbohydrate 8g, fat 7g, saturated fat 2.1g, fibre 2g, added sugar none, salt 0.18g

This is also delicious as a topping for crostini or bruschetta, with a thick slice of fresh mozzarella. Use any leftover juices as a salad dressing.

Roasted Pepper Salad

6 large red or yellow peppers,
halved and seeded
3 garlic cloves, finely chopped
small bunch fresh flatleaf parsley,
finely chopped
5 tbsp extra virgin olive oil

Takes 35 minutes, plus standing •
Serves 6

1 Preheat the grill, then grill the peppers, skin-side up, until they become blackened and blistered. Remove the peppers and put into a plastic bag. Close the bag with a knot and leave to cool.

2 Take the peppers out of the bag and peel off the blackened skin with the blunt side of a knife blade so you don't tear the flesh. Cut the peppers into strips and lay them overlapping on a large plate. (They can be covered and chilled for up to 24 hours.)

3 Scatter the peppers with the garlic and parsley, then sprinkle with the olive oil and seasoning. Leave for an hour or so to allow the flavours to develop before serving.

• Per serving 139 kcalories, protein 2g, carbohydrate 11g, fat 10g, saturated fat 1g, fibre 3g, added sugar none, salt 0.27g

Use a fruity, good-quality olive oil to bring out the full flavour
of this refreshing salad.

Tomato and Mint Salad

400g/14oz cherry tomatoes
1 small red onion
handful of mint leaves
extra virgin olive oil, for drizzling
1–2 tsp finely grated lemon zest

Takes 10 minutes • Serves 6

1 Halve the cherry tomatoes and scatter over a large serving plate.
2 Finely chop the onion and tear up the mint leaves. Throw the onion and mint over the tomatoes. (The salad will keep, covered, for 3–4 hours.)
3 Just before serving, drizzle with olive oil, season and sprinkle over the lemon zest.

• Per serving 62 kcalories, protein 1g, carbohydrate 3g, fat 5g, saturated fat 1g, fibre 1g, added sugar none, salt 0.02g

These salads look pretty served in individual glasses, and they're perfect for a casual, help-yourself party.

Solo Salads

50g/2oz pine nuts
2 × 110g bags salad leaves (such as bistro salad with red chard)
200g/8oz cherry tomatoes, roughly chopped
200g/8oz black olives

FOR THE DRESSING
1 tbsp pesto
1 tbsp lemon juice
5 tbsp olive oil

Takes 20 minutes • Serves 8

1 Make the dressing – mix the pesto and lemon juice in a small bowl. Slowly whisk in the olive oil to form a smooth emulsion and season to taste.

2 Heat a small frying pan, tip in the nuts and cook for 2–3 minutes, tossing them frequently until they are nicely browned.

3 Put the leaves in a large bowl with the tomatoes and olives. Pour in the dressing and mix well, then divide between eight glasses and sprinkle with the toasted pine nuts.

• Per serving 145 kcalories, protein 2g, carbohydrate 2g, fat 15g, saturated fat 2g, fibre 1.4g, added sugar none, salt 1.46g

You can cook the onions and mix the dressing the day before
to make this salad even easier to put together.

Parsley, Radish and Red Onion Salad

1 large red onion
1 tbsp olive oil
1 large bunch (about 50g/2oz) curly
parsley
1 bunch (about 25g/1oz) flatleaf
parsley
1 bunch radishes

FOR THE DRESSING
1 tbsp balsamic vinegar
1 tsp Dijon mustard
3 tbsp extra virgin olive oil
2 tbsp groundnut or vegetable oil

Takes 25–35 minutes • Serves 4

1 Cut the onion into thin slices. Heat the oil in a frying pan over a high heat. Tip in the onion and fry for 4–5 minutes, stirring almost constantly to break up the rings. When the onion is soft, remove the pan from the heat and leave the onion to cool.
2 Strip off the little sprigs of parsley, discarding the stalks. Slice the radishes finely.
3 For the dressing, pour the vinegar into a small jug, add the mustard and season well. Whisk thoroughly to combine, then pour in the oils and continue whisking to a thickish emulsion. Toss the parsley, radishes and onion together; pour over enough dressing to coat the leaves finely. Serve immediately.

• Per serving 173 kcalories, protein 1g, carbohydrate 4g, fat 17g, saturated fat 3g, fibre 1g, added sugar none, salt 0.11g

A crisp and crunchy salad,
that's low in fat too.

Fennel and Celery Salad

1 large or 2 small fennel bulbs
6 celery sticks
3–4 tbsp fruity extra virgin olive oil
2 tbsp lemon juice

Takes 15 minutes • Serves 6

1 Very finely slice the fennel lengthways
(a mandolin makes this much easier).
2 Cut the celery sticks into thin matchsticks.
Scatter the fennel and celery on a large plate
or platter.
3 Drizzle over the oil and lemon juice and
season. Scatter any fennel fronds and celery
leaves over if you have them.

• Per serving 57 kcalories, protein 1g, carbohydrate
1g, fat 6g, saturated fat 1g, fibre 1g, added sugar
none, salt 0.07g

This salad is perfect for a picnic – keep the raw and cooked vegetables separate en route to keep it at its crunchy, fresh best.

Spinach, Bean and Tomato Salad

FOR THE DRESSING
½ tsp French mustard
1 tbsp white wine vinegar, plus a little more to taste if necessary
4 tbsp mild light olive oil
3 tbsp double cream
1 shallot, very finely chopped
1 small garlic clove, very finely chopped
2 tbsp finely chopped fresh mint or chives

FOR THE SALAD
500g/1lb 2oz fine green beans, stalk ends trimmed
1 tbsp olive oil
450g/1lb tomatoes
100g/4oz baby spinach leaves

Takes 20 minutes • Serves 6–8

1 Put all the dressing ingredients in a screw-top jar and shake vigorously to combine. Season to taste, and add more vinegar if necessary.

2 Cook the beans in plenty of boiling salted water until just tender (about 4–5 minutes). Drain, then toss in a bowl with the olive oil and some seasoning. Cool for 5 minutes, then toss in the dressing.

3 Cut the tomatoes into wedges, quarters or halves depending on size (halved cherry tomatoes work particularly well). Toss together all the ingredients just before serving.

• Per serving for six 159 kcalories, protein 3g, carbohydrate 6g, fat 14g, saturated fat 3.6g, fibre 3g, added sugar none, salt 0.12g

Cook the beans and the garlic in advance so that you can whip up this fresh and tasty salad in minutes.

Minted Green Bean Salad

600g/1lb 5oz green beans, trimmed
3 tbsp olive oil
2 fat garlic cloves, thinly sliced
1 tbsp balsamic vinegar
3 tbsp chopped fresh mint

Takes 30 minutes • Serves 6

1 Cook the beans in boiling salted water for 5–6 minutes, until just tender, then drain and refresh under cold running water. Shake well to remove excess water, then pat dry with kitchen paper.

2 Heat 1 tablespoon of the oil in a small pan, add the garlic and fry quickly until crisp and lightly golden. Tip into a bowl with the oil from the pan and leave to cool.

3 Whisk together the remaining oil, the vinegar, mint and some seasoning. Pour over the beans and mix well. Tip into a serving bowl and scatter over the garlic in its oil.

• Per serving 79 kcalories, protein 2g, carbohydrate 4g, fat 6g, saturated fat 1g, fibre 2g, added sugar none, salt none

The fresh summer flavours of this salad make it the perfect accompaniment to a barbecue meal.

Easy Italian Bean Salad

1 bunch spring onions
2 garlic cloves
1 red chilli
2 × 400g cans cannellini beans,
drained and rinsed
400g can butter beans, drained
and rinsed
6 tbsp olive oil
2 tbsp white wine vinegar
handful of parsley, chopped

Takes 10 minutes • Serves 8

1 Finely chop the spring onions, crush the garlic and seed and finely chop the chilli.
2 Mix together with the cannellini and butter beans. Whisk the oil and vinegar together with plenty of seasoning.
3 Stir the dressing into the bean mixture with the chopped parsley and serve.

• Per serving 168 kcalories, protein 7g, carbohydrate 16g, fat 9g, saturated fat 1.2g, fibre 4.9g, added sugar none, salt 0.96g

A splash of lemon adds punch to these mildly spiced carrots.

Warm Carrot Salad with Cumin Dressing

2 tsp cumin seeds
750g/1lb 10oz carrots, cut into short sticks
2 tbsp extra virgin olive oil
4 tbsp lemon juice
4 tsp light muscovado sugar
2 garlic cloves, thinly sliced
½ tsp paprika
handful of chopped coriander
finely grated zest of 1 lemon

Takes 25 minutes • Serves 4

1 Put the cumin seeds in a dry frying pan over a lowish heat. Cook for a few minutes, tossing in the pan, until they smell fragrant and have darkened slightly. Grind them in a spice or coffee grinder.

2 Put the carrots in a saucepan and cover with cold water. Add a little salt, then bring to the boil. Lower the heat and simmer gently for 3–4 minutes. Drain.

3 Whisk the oil, lemon juice and sugar, then stir in the garlic and ¼ teaspoon salt. Stir in the cumin and paprika. Mix well with the carrots, then leave to cool, stirring occasionally. Toss in the coriander and lemon zest. Serve at room temperature.

• Per serving 141 kcalories, protein 2g, carbohydrate 20g, fat 7g, saturated fat 1g, fibre 4g, added sugar 5g, salt 0.1g

This simple, zesty side salad goes really well
with fish or lamb.

Lemon and Coriander Couscous

250g/9oz couscous
300ml/½ pint hot vegetable stock
finely grated zest of 1 lemon
2 × 20g packs fresh coriander,
chopped
handful of raisins
4 tbsp pine nuts, toasted
olive oil, for drizzling

Takes 15 minutes • Serves 4

1 Put the couscous in a large bowl, pour over the boiling stock and stir. Cover and leave for 4 minutes. Fluff up the couscous with a fork.
2 Stir in the lemon zest, coriander, raisins and pine nuts.
3 Season and drizzle with plenty of olive oil.

• Per serving 367 kcalories, protein 6g, carbohydrate 43g, fat 20g, saturated fat 3g, fibre 1g, added sugar none, salt 0.03g

Perfect served with grilled meat or fish,
fresh from the barbecue.

Thrill-of-the-grill Couscous

250g/9oz couscous
300ml/½ pint hot vegetable stock
– made with a cube is fine
250g pack cherry tomatoes
175g/6oz chestnut mushrooms
½ bunch spring onions
2 tbsp olive oil
3–4 tbsp green pesto
handful of toasted nuts, such as
pine nuts, almonds or
roughly chopped hazelnuts
good handful of basil

Takes 25–35 minutes •
Serves 4 generously

1 Put the couscous in a heatproof bowl and pour over the boiling stock. Cover with cling film and set aside to soak for 4 minutes only.
2 Halve the tomatoes and finely chop the mushrooms and spring onions. After the couscous has soaked, fork it through to break up any lumps, then stir in the oil and pesto to your taste.
3 Tip in all the vegetables and the nuts, then tear in the basil leaves. Taste and season if necessary. (This keeps in the fridge for up to a day.)

• Per serving 291 kcalories, protein 7g, carbohydrate 29g, fat 17g, saturated fat 4g, fibre 1g, added sugar none, salt 0.49g

This dish, full of wonderful flavours, is a simple and colourful addition to a buffet meal.

Asian Rice Salad

½ small bunch each mint, flatleaf parsley and coriander
2 garlic cloves, chopped
2.5cm/1in piece fresh root ginger, peeled and roughly chopped
4 tbsp soy sauce
juice of 2 limes
2 tbsp clear honey
5–6 tbsp sunflower oil
500g packet basmati rice
2 courgettes
½ bunch spring onions

Takes 40 minutes •
Serves 10 (easily halved)

1 Put the herbs, garlic and ginger in a food processor with the soy sauce, lime juice and honey. Blitz until all the ingredients are nicely chopped. Slowly drizzle in enough sunflower oil to give you a lovely, glossy emulsion. Set aside.

2 Cook the rice according to the packet instructions. Meanwhile, finely dice the courgettes and finely slice the spring onions at an angle.

3 Drain the rice, cool quickly, then stir in the courgettes, spring onions and dressing. (If made ahead, the salad can be refrigerated overnight.)

• Per serving 235 kcalories, protein 5g, carbohydrate 44g, fat 6g, saturated fat 0.7g, fibre 0.3g, added sugar 2.4g, salt 1.09g

Adding the lemony olive oil dressing to the just-cooked potatoes and beans means that all the fresh flavours are absorbed as they cool.

New Potato Salad with Herb Dressing

700g/1lb 9oz new potatoes, scrubbed
175g/6oz green beans, cut into 5cm/2in lengths

FOR THE DRESSING
3 tbsp extra virgin olive oil
grated zest and juice of 1 small lemon
2 tbsp chopped fresh mint
1 tbsp chopped fresh parsley
1 tbsp snipped fresh chervil or chives

Takes 30 minutes • Serves 4

1 Bring a pan of salted water to the boil. Add the potatoes and boil for 8 minutes. Tip in the beans and cook for a further 4–5 minutes, or until the potatoes and beans are both just tender.
2 Meanwhile, whisk all the dressing ingredients together. Season well.
3 Drain the beans and potatoes and cut the potatoes in half. Toss with the dressing while still hot. Cover and chill until ready to serve. Bring to room temperature before serving.

• Per serving 220 kcalories, protein 5g, carbohydrate 32g, fat 9g, saturated fat 1g, fibre 3g, added sugar none, salt 0.04g

New potatoes are usually so clean you don't need to scrub them.
Don't bother to peel them as the skin adds fibre.

Cracked Potato Salad

750g/1lb 10oz small new potatoes
4 tbsp white wine
2 tbsp olive oil
1 small red onion, thinly sliced
3 tbsp roughly chopped fresh parsley

Takes 25 minutes • Serves 4

1 Cook the potatoes in boiling salted water for about 15 minutes until tender. Drain and return them to the pan.

2 Lightly bash each potato with a masher or fork so they are cracked but still whole. Return to the heat and pour in the wine. Boil fiercely for 2–3 minutes until most of the wine has evaporated.

3 Stir in the olive oil, the sliced onion and chopped parsley. Season and toss everything together before serving.

• Per serving 197 kcalories, protein 3g, carbohydrate 32g, fat 6g, saturated fat 0.8g, fibre 2.3g, added sugar none, salt 0.06g

If you're having a party, make this mildly spiced salad in advance to save you time and hassle on the day.

Potato Salad with Curried Mayo

1.25kg/2¾lb salad potatoes, such as Charlotte, halved if large
1 bunch spring onions
1 tbsp groundnut or sunflower oil
1 tsp black mustard seeds, plus extra to serve
1 tbsp Madras curry paste
200g carton low-fat natural yogurt
4 tbsp mayonnaise
4 celery sticks, thickly sliced

Takes 30 minutes •
Serves 8 (easily halved)

1 Cook the potatoes in boiling salted water for 15 minutes until tender. Drain and cool. Trim the spring onions, then slice the white bulb ends. Reserve the green stems.

2 Heat the oil in a deep saucepan, add the mustard seeds and cook until they pop. Stir in the sliced spring onions and curry paste and keep stirring for 2 minutes. Tip the mixture into a large bowl, then stir in the yogurt, mayonnaise and some seasoning. Chop all but two of the green spring onion stems. Stir into the dressing with the potatoes and celery.

3 Pile the salad into a serving bowl. Cut the remaining spring onion stems into long shreds and scatter them over the salad along with a few mustard seeds.

• Per serving 204 kcalories, protein 5g, carbohydrate 28g, fat 9g, saturated fat 1g, fibre 2g, added sugar none, salt 0.29g

Choose potatoes that are firm and evenly sized so that some aren't overcooked before the others are done.

Salsa Potato Salad

350g/12oz new potatoes, halved
1 small garlic clove
3 spring onions
small handful each of mint and parsley
2 tbsp olive oil

Takes 20 minutes •
Serves 2 (easily doubled)

1 Cook the potatoes in boiling salted water for about 10–15 minutes until tender.
2 Meanwhile, roughly chop the garlic and the spring onions and put in a food processor with the herbs. Whizz together until finely chopped, then add the oil and 2 tablespoons water. Whizz again with some seasoning.
3 Drain the potatoes and toss with the herb salsa. Serve warm, or leave to cool.

• Per serving 228 kcalories, protein 4g, carbohydrate 29g, fat 12g, saturated fat 1.6g, fibre 2.1g, added sugar none, salt 0.05g

Eat this healthy winter salad as soon as it's made if you like your cabbage crispy and crunchy.

Sesame Slaw

½ white cabbage, finely shredded
2 carrots, grated
2cm/¾in piece fresh root ginger, peeled and grated
1 plump red chilli (seeds removed if you like), chopped
finely grated zest and juice of 1 orange
1 tbsp lemon juice
1 tbsp sesame seeds
1 tbsp each sesame and groundnut or vegetable oil
1–2 tsp light muscovado sugar

Takes 20 minutes • Serves 4

1 Tip the cabbage into a large bowl and mix with the carrots, ginger, chilli, orange zest and juice and lemon juice.
2 Put the sesame seeds in a small dry pan and heat briefly until golden, shaking the pan often so they don't burn.
3 Toss the sesame seeds into the cabbage with the oils, some seasoning and sugar to taste before serving.

• Per serving 119 kcalories, protein 2g, carbohydrate 10g, fat 8g, saturated fat 1.2g, fibre 3g, added sugar 1.3g, salt 0.05g

Marinating the strawberries in the Beaujolais gives them a lovely flavour, but don't do it too far ahead or they will lose their texture.

Beaujolais Strawberry Salad

700g/1lb 9oz strawberries, hulled and halved
3 tbsp golden caster sugar
handful of mint leaves, plus a few extra
½ bottle Beaujolais

Takes 5 minutes, plus marinating • Serves 6

1 Lay the strawberries in a bowl and sprinkle over the caster sugar.
2 Scatter over a handful of mint leaves and let the strawberries sit for about 30 minutes so they start to release their juices.
3 Pour over the Beaujolais, scatter over a few more fresh mint leaves, leave for another 10 minutes, then serve.

• Per serving 102 kcalories, protein 1g, carbohydrate 15g, fat 1g, saturated fat none, fibre 1g, added sugar 8g, salt 0.03g

Turn fresh summer berries into a stylish, but simple dessert
with a flavoured syrup.

Summer Fruits with Lemon Syrup

100g/4oz golden caster sugar
1 lemongrass stalk
2 strips lemon zest (peeled with
a vegetable peeler)
500g/1lb 2oz mixed summer fruits,
such as strawberries,
raspberries and redcurrants

Takes 10 minutes, plus steeping •
Serves 4

1 Stir 250ml/9fl oz boiling water and the
sugar together until the sugar has dissolved.
2 Bruise the lemongrass with a rolling pin
to release the flavour, then add to the syrup
with the lemon zest. Leave to cool. (This
can keep in a jar in the fridge for 2–3 days.)
3 Pour the syrup over the fruit, stir to mix,
then leave to steep for about 30 minutes
before serving.

• Per serving 130 kcalories, protein 1g, carbohydrate
33g, fat none, saturated fat none, fibre 2.7g, added
sugar 26.3g, salt 0.02g

Make the most of summer fruits with this refreshing, low-fat pudding.

Liqueur Oranges with Red Berries

6 oranges
2–3 tbsp Grand Marnier
1–2 tbsp golden caster sugar, to taste
400g punnet strawberries, hulled and halved
125g punnet raspberries
few mint sprigs and icing sugar, to serve

Takes 25 minutes, plus marinating • Serves 4

1 Slice the peel and all the pith from 4 of the oranges with a sharp knife. Cut the oranges into slices, collecting the juice, remove any pips, then put the orange slices in a serving bowl with the juices.

2 Squeeze the juice from the remaining oranges and pour over the sliced oranges with the Grand Marnier and sugar to taste. Toss together, then add the strawberries and raspberries, being careful not to squash the raspberries. Leave for about 30 minutes, then serve scattered with the mint leaves and a sifting of icing sugar.

• Per serving 162 kcalories, protein 4g, carbohydrate 34g, fat none, saturated fat none, fibre 6g, added sugar 5.6g, salt 0.05g

A fantastic instant dessert that's a great way to eat more fruit.
And it's even better for you if you use low-fat yogurt.

Fruit Salad with Chocolate Dip

50g/2oz dark chocolate
125g carton plain, raspberry or
strawberry yogurt
chunks of pineapple and crisp apple
or pear, orange segments
and grapes

Takes 10 minutes • Serves 2

1 Melt the chocolate in a bowl over hot water (or in the microwave).
2 Stir the chocolate into the yogurt until smooth. Arrange the fruits together on a platter.
3 Serve the fresh fruit salad with the yogurt for dipping.

• Per serving 246 kcalories, protein 6g, carbohydrate 38g, fat 9g, saturated fat 5.2g, fibre 2.4g, added sugar 15.6g, salt 0.14g

Lemongrass adds an intriguing citrus taste and fragrance to the syrup for this exotic fruit salad. It's delicious served with mango sorbet.

Tropical Fruits with Lemongrass

425g can lychees in syrup
2 lemongrass stalks, halved and bashed with a rolling pin
85g/3oz caster sugar
800g/1¾lb mix of prepared tropical fruits, such as papaya, mango, pineapple, melon
100g/4oz seedless red grapes
6 macaroons or coconut biscuits, to serve

Takes 15 minutes, plus chilling • Serves 6

1 Drain the lychees' juice into a pan and put the lychees in a large serving bowl. Add the lemongrass and sugar to the pan.
2 Heat gently until the sugar dissolves, then boil for 1 minute. Turn off the heat and set aside – the lemongrass will add flavour as it cools.
3 Strain the syrup over the lychees and tip in the prepared fruits. Chill. Serve with macaroons or coconut biscuits.

• Per serving 172 kcalories, protein 1g, carbohydrate 44g, fat none, saturated fat none, fibre 3g, added sugar 18g, salt 0.02g

Try this fresh twist on fruit salad.

Exotic Fruits with Gingery Fromage Frais

425ml/¾ pint unsweetened
apple juice
3 tbsp clear honey
juice of 1 lime or ½ lemon
2 mangoes, peeled, stoned and sliced
2 papayas, peeled, seeded and sliced
3 kiwi fruit, peeled and cut
into wedges
1 small charentais or cantaloupe
melon, peeled and cut into chunks
500g carton low-fat plain
fromage frais
2 pieces stem ginger in syrup,
finely chopped
2 tbsp syrup from the jar of ginger

Takes 35 minutes, plus cooling •
Serves 6

1 Put the apple juice, honey and lime or lemon juice into a saucepan. Bring it up to the boil, turn the heat down to low and simmer gently for 15–20 minutes until the liquid has reduced slightly.
2 Pour into a serving dish and leave to cool for 5–10 minutes. Mix all the fruit in with the warm syrup and leave to cool.
3 While the fruit is cooling, mix together the fromage frais, chopped ginger and ginger syrup. Cover and chill until ready to serve. Serve the fruit salad with the fromage frais.

• Per serving 201 kcalories, protein 8g, carbohydrate 43g, fat 1g, saturated fat none, fibre 4g, added sugar 8g, salt 0.11g

Vary the fruit according to what's available.
This salad is especially good with ice cream in the summer.

Spiced Fruit Salad

1 papaya
1 mango
4 plums
1 star fruit
1 small pineapple

FOR THE SPICED SYRUP
3 star anise
1 vanilla pod, split lengthways
finely grated zest of ½ lemon and
½ lime
1 cinnamon stick
4 cloves
200g/8oz golden caster sugar

Takes 35 minutes, plus chilling •
Serves 6

1 Put all the syrup ingredients in a heavy-based saucepan with 600ml/1 pint water. Simmer gently for about 15 minutes, stirring occasionally as the sugar dissolves. Allow the syrup to cool, then pour into a large serving bowl.

2 Peel, seed and slice the papaya. Peel, stone and slice the mango and plums; slice the star fruit. Peel, core and slice the pineapple.

3 Tip all the fruits into the syrup. Cover and chill for at least an hour before serving.

• Per serving 226 kcalories, protein 1g, carbohydrate 58g, fat none, saturated fat none, fibre 4.1g, added sugar 35g, salt 0.02g

This speedy dessert makes the
perfect end to a spicy meal.

Minty Mango Salad

3 mangoes
3 tbsp Cointreau
handful of fresh mint leaves,
shredded

Takes 10 minutes • Serves 6

1 Peel the mangoes and carefully slice off
each fleshly side close to the stone. Slice
the mango flesh.
2 Splash with the Cointreau, then cover
and chill for at least 2 hours (or overnight).
3 Serve straight from the fridge, showered
with the shredded mint leaves.

• Per serving 81 kcalories, protein 1g, carbohydrate
16g, fat none, saturated fat none, fibre 3g, added
sugar 2g, salt 0.01g

A simple healthy dessert that makes the most
of just three ingredients.

Papaya with Lime and Blueberries

2 papayas
2 limes
2 handfuls of blueberries

Takes 5 minutes • Serves 4

1 Halve the papayas lengthways. Scoop out and discard the seeds and sit the papaya halves on serving plates.
2 Squeeze the juice from 1½ limes. Cut the remaining ½ lime into four wedges.
3 Pour the lime juice over the papaya halves, scatter the blueberries over and serve.

• Per serving 59 kcalories, protein 1g, carbohydrate 14g, fat none, saturated fat none, fibre 3.6g, added sugar none, salt 0.02g

Make a big batch to last a week and have it for breakfast every day – the flavours will get even better as the week goes on.

Winter Fruit Salad

600g/1lb 5oz good-quality ready-to-eat dried fruits (such as prunes, pears, apricots, figs and cranberries)
3 tbsp clear honey
1 vanilla pod, split lengthways
1 Earl Grey tea bag
1 tbsp fresh lemon juice
Greek yogurt, to serve

Takes 25 minutes, plus infusing and chilling • Serves 6

1 Tip the fruits and 700ml/1¼ pints cold water into a large saucepan. Add the honey and vanilla, scraping the seeds from the pod into the pan. Bring to the boil. Stir well, lower the heat and simmer for 10 minutes until slightly syrupy.
2 Take the pan off the heat and stir in the tea bag. Leave to infuse for 10 minutes.
3 Discard the tea bag and vanilla pod, tip the fruits and liquid into a non-metallic bowl and pour over the lemon juice. Stir, then leave to cool. Cover and chill. (It will keep for 3–4 days.) Serve with Greek yogurt.

• Per serving 192 kcalories, protein 3g, carbohydrate 46g, fat 1g, saturated fat none, fibre 6g, added sugar 6g, salt 0.07g

You can use grapefruit juice instead of orange if you prefer.
Any leftovers make a great breakfast.

Spicy Winter Fruit Compote

500g pack mixed dried fruit
200ml/7fl oz fresh orange juice
½ cinnamon stick
6 cloves
6 black peppercorns
0%-fat Greek yogurt or low-fat
fromage frais, to serve

Takes 5–10 minutes • Serves 4

1 Tip the dried fruit, orange juice and whole spices into a microwave-proof bowl. Microwave on High for 4–5 minutes, stirring halfway through, until the juices become sticky and the fruits are plump.
2 Leave the compote to stand for a minute and serve in bowls with spoonfuls of Greek yogurt or fromage frais.

• Per serving 352 kcalories, protein 3g, carbohydrate 89g, fat 1g, saturated fat none, fibre 3g, added sugar none, salt 0.15g

Index

Picture credits and recipe credits

BBC Worldwide would like to thank the following for providing photographs. While every effort has been made to trace and acknowledge all photographers, we would like to apologize should there be any errors or omissions.

Marie-Louise Avery p43, p179, p183, p187; Iain Bagwell p55, p61, p67, p71; Steve Baxter p117, p147; John Bennett p19; Linda Burgess p141; Pete Cassidy p159, p165, p205; Jean Cazals p171, p203; Ken Field p49, p51, p65, p73, p85; William Lingwood p37, p69, p87, p125, p145; David Munns p11, p21, p23, p27, p31, p91, p93, p95, p105, p129, p131, p139, p151, p153, p199, p201, p207; Myles New p59, p135; Michael Paul p17, p29, p103, p127, p185; Juliet Piddington p39, p53, p195; Craig Robertson p15, p161, p167, p197, p209; Roger Stowell p13, p25, p57, p63, p77, p79, p83, p101, p107, p119, p133, p137, p149, p169, p177; Martin Thompson p163; Simon Walton p81; Philip Webb p35, p41, p47, p89, p121, p143, p175, p193, p211; Simon Wheeler p33, p45, p97, p99, p109, p111, p113, p115, p123, p181, p191; Geoff Wilkinson p75, p155, p157; Peter Williams p173, p189.

All the recipes in this book have been created by the editorial team on *BBC Good Food Magazine*:

Lorna Brash, Sara Buenfeld, Mary Cadogan, Barney Desmazery, Kate Moseley, Orlando Murrin, Vicky Musselman, Angela Nilsen, Maggie Pannell, Jenny White, Jeni Wright.